Please Help My Mummy

BABY FELIX HAS BEEN ABANDONED,
BUT CAN THE TRUTH BE DISCOVERED
IN TIME TO HELP HIS MUM?

MAGGIE HARTLEY

WITH
HEATHER BISHOP

SEVEN DIALS

First published in Great Britain in 2025 by Seven Dials,
an imprint of The Orion Publishing Group Ltd
Carmelite House, 50 Victoria Embankment
London EC4Y 0DZ

An Hachette UK Company

The authorised representative in the EEA is Hachette Ireland,
8 Castlecourt Centre, Dublin 15, D15 XTP3, Ireland
(email: info@hbgi.ie)

1 3 5 7 9 10 8 6 4 2

A CIP catalogue record for this book is
available from the British Library.

ISBN (Mass Market Paperback) 978 1 3996 2922 5
ISBN (Ebook) 978 1 3996 2923 2
ISBN (Audio) 978 1 3996 2924 9

Typeset by Born Group
Printed and bound in Great Britain by Clays Ltd, Elcograf S.p.A.

MIX
Paper | Supporting
responsible forestry
FSC
www.fsc.org
FSC® C104740

www.orionbooks.co.uk

Please Help My Mummy

Also by Maggie Hartley

Dedication

This book is dedicated to Felix and Amena and all the children who have passed through my home. It's been a privilege to have cared for you and to be able to share your stories. And to the children who live with me now: thank you for your determination, strength and joy, and for sharing your lives with me.

Contents

A Message from Maggie

I wanted to write this book to give people an honest account about what it's like to be a foster carer, to talk about some of the challenges that I face on a day-to-day basis and about some of the children that I've helped.

My main concern throughout all this is to protect the children who have been in my care. For this reason, all names and identifying details have been changed, including my own, and no locations have been included.

Being a foster carer is a privilege and I couldn't imagine doing anything else. My house is never quiet but I wouldn't have it any other way. I hope perhaps my stories will inspire other people to consider fostering as new carers are always desperately needed. In fact, there's currently a recruitment crisis facing the foster community – across the UK there's currently a shortage of 6,500 foster families. It comes at the same time as the number of children in care in the UK exceeds 100,000 – the highest on record.[*] Foster carers are needed more than ever, so please do look into it if it's something that you or someone you know has ever considered.

---

[*] Figures and information from The Fostering Network. 'More children to end up in unsuitable homes if more foster carers aren't urgently recruited', 13 May 2024. Available at: https://www.thefosteringnetwork.org.uk/media-release/2024/more-children-end-unsuitable-homes-if-more-foster-carers-arent-urgently (accessed 7 November 2024).

The Bag on the Platform

Melissa wearily walked up the platform to her usual spot at the top end. She did this journey at 6.50 a.m. every day, so she knew exactly where to stand so the doors of the first carriage opened right in front of her and she had the best chance of getting a seat on the train.

Melissa was a nurse on a geriatric ward so she cherished the relative peace and quiet of her twenty-minute commute before she walked through the doors of the busy hospital, knowing it would be at least another twelve hours before she could walk back out of them again.

She was still lost in her thoughts as she walked to the end of the platform, her eyes half closed as the warmth of the spring sun shone on her face.

She could only see one other person waiting there – a woman with long dark hair sitting on one of the seats. But as Melissa walked towards her, the woman suddenly jumped up and brushed past her. Head down, she almost broke into a jog as she dashed back along the platform towards the station entrance.

That's a bit odd, Melissa thought to herself. Maybe the woman had decided she didn't want to catch the train after all? It was a thought Melissa was quite envious of. Part of her wished she could head home and have a leisurely breakfast with her husband Dave, and nine-year-old daughter Kayleigh, instead of creeping out the door while they were both still asleep.

Melissa walked towards the row of seats where the woman had been sitting as she wanted to get her book out. But as she put her rucksack down on one of the seats, she noticed a large holdall on the floor.

She'd left her bag.

Melissa quickly spun around but as she looked down the platform, she could see the woman had gone.

She sighed. She'd have to take the forgotten holdall to the ticket office at the front of the station and would probably miss her train. But her conscience wouldn't let her leave the bag there. What if someone less honest than herself stumbled across it and took it?

But, before she could start to reach towards the large bag, Melissa froze.

There was something moving.

Then she heard a noise that chilled her to the bone.

A loud cry.

It was the sort of distinctive wail that only came from one thing.

As she looked inside the unzipped bag, she couldn't believe what she was seeing. It was a newborn baby.

'What the hell?' she gasped.

The baby was tiny; Melissa guessed it was no more than a few weeks old. It was dressed in a yellow knitted cardigan and had a hat and little mittens on. It was wrapped in a blue woollen blanket, and pinned to it was a handwritten note. The writing was small and neat.

My name is Felix Oliver. Please look after me.

Still not quite believing what she was seeing, Melissa bent down and carefully lifted the baby boy out of the bag and into her arms.

'There, there,' she shushed, wrapping the blanket around him to protect him from the cold. 'You're OK.'

The baby looked up at Melissa with big blue eyes. He was absolutely perfect, and looked clean and well-cared-for. There was a sheepskin blanket in the base of the bag and a fluffy white rabbit; someone had obviously wanted to make sure that he was as warm as possible.

Maybe that's what the woman had been doing – waiting until someone had come along so she was sure that the baby would be found and not out in the cold on his own for too long?

What on earth possessed someone to leave a newborn at a train station? Melissa hadn't paid much attention to the woman as she had been walking quickly with her head down. But she knew, from what little she'd seen, that she wasn't a teenager or a young girl. She was definitely a woman, a well-dressed one at that.

The baby let out another cry and squirmed in Melissa's arms.

'It's OK, Felix,' she soothed. 'Don't worry, we're going to find your mummy.'

She set off down the platform to get the station staff to call the police and find out who the baby belonged to – and why on earth he'd been abandoned.

ONE

A Full House

Crawling through a narrow inflatable tunnel trying to catch up with a toddler wasn't exactly my idea of fun for a Friday morning.

'Edie,' I puffed. 'Wait for Nana.'

'Come on, Nana,' she sighed, clearly not happy that I was crawling along at a snail's pace.

'I'm trying, lovey, I'm trying,' I said as a couple of speedy toddlers pushed past me.

I finally got to the end of the tunnel to find a slide leading to a ball pit.

'Look at the slide,' grinned Edie.

I knew it was her favourite and although I didn't fancy whizzing down it at lightning speed into a pit of sticky plastic balls, I would have done anything for three-year-old Edie.

I had the whole day with her while her mum, my foster daughter Louisa, had some time off with her husband, Charlie. One of Charlie's cousins was getting married and I'd said I'd look after Edie so they could relax and enjoy themselves.

They were staying overnight in a hotel and coming to pick Edie up in the morning.

Louisa was as close to me as any biological child could be. She'd come to live with me as a teenager after her parents tragically died in a car crash and had stayed with me until marrying Charlie. They owned their own flat a short drive from my house.

Edie called me Nana and I cherished the role, and absolutely adored my little granddaughter. So much so, I'd agreed to take her to her favourite soft-play centre.

Finally, I manoeuvred myself into position at the top of the slide and Edie plonked herself on my knee.

'One, two, three,' she counted as I pushed us off. 'Wheeee!'

Edie squealed as we landed with a thump in the ball pit, quickly jumping up while I struggled to get my balance.

'Again, Nana!' she grinned.

We'd been there for nearly three hours and I knew Edie must be starting to get hungry. I'd certainly had enough of soft play for now.

'Let's get some lunch, flower,' I told her. 'Would you like to go to the café?'

Edie nodded excitedly.

'Sausage roll?' she asked me.

'Yes, you can have a sausage roll,' I smiled. 'And a chocolate crispy cake.'

That was enough to persuade her. Two minutes later, Edie was running towards the table where my bag was.

'Meena coming too?' she asked me, as I helped her to get her shoes on.

'No, Amena's at school, lovey,' I told her. 'But you'll see her later, back at my house.'

Amena was the sixteen-year-old that I'd been fostering for well over a year. She and her mum, Hodan, were from Somalia but they'd been in the UK for several years. Hodan had had to go to France to nurse her sister through cancer treatment. Unfortunately, after surgery and treatment, the illness was now terminal and Hodan was supporting her sister through palliative care. Hodan hadn't wanted to take Amena out of school during her GCSEs and with no family in the UK, she had come to stay with me. Although she missed her mum terribly, they spoke on the phone every day and saw each other when Hodan came back to the UK every few months.

Amena was such a sweet girl. She always helped out with any other foster children I was looking after and I'd grown really fond of her.

'And you'll see Shola and Jordan too,' I told Edie.

She nodded. Shola and Jordan were a sister and brother who were ten and eight respectively. They'd been with their foster carer, Maria, since they were toddlers. But Maria had had to have an operation on her back, so they'd been living with me while Maria was looked after at home by her husband. So, for the past few weeks, I'd had a very full house as three was the maximum number of children that I was allowed to foster at any one time.

I weaved my way through the packed café to the table where Edie was already sitting, a full tray balanced precariously in my hands.

It was a miracle I hadn't dropped anything, I thought to myself, as I gave Edie her apple juice and sausage roll, and placed down my tea and jacket potato with beans.

I'd finally put the empty tray down when I felt my mobile ringing in my bag.

'Phone, Nana,' nodded Edie.

'I know, flower,' I smiled. 'I'll get it in a minute.'

But by the time I'd sat down and got myself sorted, I'd missed the call.

I delved into my bag and got out my mobile. I could see from the name on the screen that the missed call was from Becky, my supervising social worker at the fostering agency I worked for. I assumed that she was ringing about Shola and Jordan. Maria had been given the OK by her consultant and was apparently ready to have them back at some point over the next few days. She was probably ringing to make arrangements.

I quickly gave her a call back.

'Hi, Becky,' I said. 'Sorry, I can't hear you that well. I'm in a café having lunch with Edie but I saw that you'd called.'

'Ah, that's nice,' Becky replied. 'How is little Edie? I haven't seen her for ages. I bet she's really growing up.'

'Oh, she is,' I smiled. 'I know I'm biased but she's a cutie.'

Edie grinned up at me as she tucked into her sausage roll, knowing full well that I was talking about her.

'I'd normally say that I'd ring you back later when you were at home, Maggie, but something's come up that I need an immediate answer on.'

'Oh, right,' I said.

This didn't sound like it was about Shola and Jordan after all.

'I know how much you love babies . . .' Becky started. 'So, I wondered how you'd feel about taking on a five-week-old?'

'Wow,' I gasped. 'What's led a tiny baby like that to end up in the care system?'

As Becky told me the story, I could hardly believe what I was hearing. She explained that earlier that morning, the baby boy had been found abandoned at a railway station.

'What?' I gasped. 'Had he been there long?'

'I honestly don't know,' she replied. 'I only have the basic details and the name and number of the social worker dealing with it.'

'Gosh,' I sighed. 'How sad. The poor mother – she must be in a desperate situation to feel that she had no other option than to do that.'

'It's not clear what the circumstances are and the police are still desperately trying to trace the mother,' continued Becky. 'Social Services need someone to look after the baby while they investigate it. I know how much you love looking after babies, but I also appreciate that it might be a bit of a squeeze with three foster children already living with you.'

I was approved to look after three children but if I took the baby on, it would mean that I would be over my limit.

'We'd have to apply for an exemption to the normal fostering numbers,' Becky told me. 'But as Shola and Jordan are likely to be going back to Maria's soon, I think it will be given.'

In order for the local authority to grant the exemption, all of the other children's social workers would have to agree to it.

It would mean I had a full house, but Amena was no trouble and Shola and Jordan were due to go back to live with Maria any day.

'What do you think?' she asked me.

'You know me, Becky,' I replied. 'I could never say no to a baby.'

'I thought that might be the case,' she laughed. 'Can I get the social worker to give you a call? Her name's Rupinder and the baby's called Felix.'

'Yes, of course,' I said. 'I should be home in half an hour or so and it will be much easier to talk then.'

'OK,' she said. 'Thanks, Maggie.'

In my entire fostering career, I don't think I'd ever said no to a baby. I just loved everything about them – the cuddles, their sweet smell and their big smiles. I didn't even mind the nappies and the sleepless nights . . .

I put the phone down and Edie grinned up at me.

'Where's the baby, Nana?' she asked. She'd obviously over-heard some of what I'd been talking about.

'The baby's coming to live at Nana's house for a little while,' I told her.

'Me like babies,' she smiled.

'I like babies too, Edie,' I replied.

As we tucked into our lunch, I couldn't get the thought of that tiny baby being left on a station platform out of my head. What on earth would lead someone to do that?

Back at home, I put on Edie's current favourite film, *Finding Nemo*, so I could chat to the social worker and hopefully start to get things ready for Felix's arrival.

I had a cot but I knew a newborn baby would be more snug in a Moses basket. Luckily, I already had one of those tucked away under my bed. Although I wasn't sure what time the social worker was going to call, I also knew that plans sometimes changed so I wanted confirmation from her that this was actually going ahead before I rushed around getting everything ready.

I was glad when my phone rang twenty minutes after we'd got back.

'Hi, it's Rupinder from Social Services,' said a youthful-sounding voice.

'Hello,' I replied. 'I was waiting for you to call. What can you tell me about Felix?'

She reiterated what Becky had said – how he'd been found in a bag on the platform of the train station.

'Is he OK?' I asked, worried as it had been such a cold morning.

'Thankfully he's absolutely fine,' Rupinder replied. 'We took him straight to A&E to get him checked out, but the paediatrician said he's a good weight and he's clearly been well looked after.'

She described how his clothes were pristine, his nappy had recently been changed and he was clean.

'From what the police said, we don't think he'd been there for long and he was well wrapped up so he wasn't cold,' she added.

'Thank goodness he was found so quickly,' I sighed. 'It's just so awful that someone would abandon their baby like that.'

'I know,' sighed Rupinder. 'The police are currently trying to trace his mum. Often with these cases, the mother has given birth in secret so there's no record of her pregnancy and birth. They're keen to make sure that she's OK.'

'But Felix is five weeks old,' I sighed. 'It's a long time to keep a baby's existence hidden and then suddenly abandon him.'

'I know, it's all very strange,' replied Rupinder.

As the police were urgently looking for his mother, my main priority now was to make sure that Felix was well cared for.

'When would you like to bring him round?' I asked.

'Well, he's currently tucking into a bottle that one of the nurses is giving him, so if it's OK with you, I'll give him a quick nappy change after that and bring him over to you.'

'That's fine,' I said.

I told her about Edie and that I already had three other foster children in my care.

'Edie's staying over tonight so I'll put her on a camp-bed in my room and then Felix in a Moses basket next to my bed.'

'You're going to have your hands full,' Rupinder told me.

'I am indeed,' I agreed.

It was going to be a very long day.

TWO

The Juggle

By the time there was a knock on the door, just over an hour later, I was as ready as I would ever be.

I'd found a packet of babygros for newborns that I'd obviously picked up in a sale and forgotten about, and I always had a stash of nappies, wipes, bottles and formula in my cupboard just in case. I had enough to tide me over until I could get to the shops in the next few days.

I also had a pram and a baby bouncer in the loft, but I hated climbing up the rickety ladder into the loft hatch myself. So I decided to wait until Louisa and Charlie came to collect Edie the following day, when I would ask them to give me a hand.

'Baby!' yelled Edie excitedly as she ran to the front door.

'Yes, that should be baby Felix,' I told her.

I opened the door to find a smiling dark-haired woman in her thirties. Edie rushed over to the car seat that was next to her on the doorstep.

'Hi, Maggie, I'm Rupinder,' she smiled, showing me her ID as all social workers always did when they first met someone new.

'Hiya,' I replied. 'Come on in.'

Edie was all over Felix; I hadn't even had a chance to look at him.

'Hello, baby,' she cooed, covering him with kisses.

'Gentle, Edie,' I told her. 'Let Rupinder bring baby Felix in and we can get him out of his car seat.'

Rupinder carried him into the hallway and I led them through to the kitchen.

'Me hold the baby?' Edie asked me.

'He's very tiny,' I told her. 'And we need to be very careful with him so I think it's best the grown-ups hold him for now.'

'Maybe you can give him a cuddle later with Maggie's help?' Rupinder suggested.

'That's a really good idea, Rupinder,' I said. 'Now, Edie, do you want to go and watch *Finding Nemo* while Rupinder and I have a chat?'

Edie nodded excitedly and ran off to the living room.

'She loves babies,' I explained. 'She was so excited when she knew Felix was coming.'

'Bless her,' she said. 'She's very sweet.'

With Edie safely out of the way, I was finally able to get a proper look at Felix. He was wide awake and very alert, and was looking around my kitchen. He had big blue eyes and wispy chestnut hair.

'Oh, he's gorgeous,' I sighed, gently stroking his cheek. 'And what a beautiful outfit.'

He was dressed in a pale blue babygro and a soft knitted yellow cardigan.

'That looks homemade,' I said.

'I think it is,' said Rupinder. 'Someone's knitted that for him as there was no label on it when the police checked. It's what he was wearing when he was found. And there's a little hat and a matching pair of mittens in here as well as a blanket.'

She opened up the plastic bag that she'd been carrying and lifted out a blue blanket with a little elephant and 'Felix' embroidered on it.

'He also came with this,' she said, showing me a white fluffy rabbit.

It was baffling. Someone had clearly cared for Felix and treasured him, so why had he been abandoned?

Rupinder explained that he'd also been found with a note asking the reader to 'please look after me'.

'Apparently he was found by a nurse,' she told me. 'The police have spoken to her and she saw who she thought was the mother leaving the scene. She got the impression that the woman had only left once she knew the baby was going to be found.'

Rupinder went on to explain that the police were doing their best to trace Felix's mum. 'It helps that we know his name although, as he's only five weeks, his birth might not have been registered yet. The police are going to try all the local hospitals and health visitors to see if they remember a baby of that name.'

She mentioned they were also going to do a media appeal and had taken photos of his blanket, rabbit and clothes in case it encouraged someone to come forward with information. They had also taken DNA samples.

'Somebody must know something,' sighed Rupinder.

I agreed. It was very hard to conceal a birth and a newborn baby for well over a month.

'And obviously, for all we know, there might be a father too,' she added. 'We can't simply assume it's just the mother who has abandoned him.'

I nodded in agreement.

'Can I have a cuddle with Felix?' I asked her.

'Of course you can,' said Rupinder.

Carefully, she lifted him out of the car seat and into my arms. He felt so light after lugging Edie around all day.

'Hello, little man,' I said. 'Are you going to be a good boy for me?'

Even though he was tiny, he felt very robust.

'He's a good weight for a newborn,' I observed.

'The paediatrician at A&E said that,' smiled Rupinder. 'He's twelve pounds so he's a chunky little thing and he's clearly been well fed.'

'So what happens now?' I asked.

'Well, while the police try to trace his mother or his parents, there isn't a lot we can do.'

The courts had issued an EPO – an emergency protection order – which meant Social Services had parental responsibility for him.

'How are you fixed for baby stuff?' asked Rupinder. 'I'm sure we have a few things in our office that we can cobble together for you.'

'That's very kind but I'm fine,' I told her. 'I've fostered lots of babies over the years so I've got the essentials. I've already got some bottles in the steriliser.'

We had a coffee and went over a few bits of paperwork.

I looked down and realised Felix was now fast asleep in my arms.

'He's a contented boy,' I sighed.

'Let's hope he stays that way,' replied Rupinder.

'Maggie, I'm going to have to head back to the office now,' she added. 'But let's keep in touch and I'll let you know if there are any developments over the weekend.'

'Thanks,' I replied. 'I'm sure we'll be fine but I'll give the duty worker a ring if there are any problems.'

I got up to see her out, Felix still fast asleep in my arms.

'Good luck,' she said. 'I hope he settles for you tonight.'

'Oh, we'll be fine,' I replied. 'We'll muddle through.'

Once I'd waved her off, I went into the living room to check on Edie.

'Baby!' she smiled as I sat down next to her on the sofa with Felix. She patted his head affectionately and bent over to give him a kiss.

'Good girl,' I smiled. 'That's really lovely and gentle.'

Just then, I heard a key in the door.

'Mena!' yelled Edie, jumping up.

Amena's face dropped when she glanced through the living-room doorway and saw the baby in my arms. She'd gone to school that morning and come home to find a baby in the house.

'Wow,' she said. 'Where did that come from?'

I explained that his name was Felix and that he'd come to stay with us for a little while. Amena had been with me long enough to know that children came and went at a moment's notice and she accepted the news calmly and walked over to peep at the baby, smiling.

A few minutes later, there was another knock at the door. I glanced at the clock and realised that it was probably Shola and Jordan. As their school was nearly a fifty-minute drive from my house, Social Services had organised a taxi for them while they were with me.

As I opened the door to them, their eyes widened at the sight of Felix in my arms.

'This is baby Felix,' I explained. 'And he's come to stay with me for a while.'

'Oh, he's small,' remarked Jordan.

Shola looked vaguely interested for a minute, but then they both put their bags down and went to watch the film with Edie. I could tell the next few days were going to be a juggling act, managing the different children's needs. However, as a foster carer I was often at capacity – as sadly there were more children in the care system than there were foster places – so I'd had to get used to caring for multiple children.

With the little ones occupied, I knew I'd better get on with dinner.

As I hadn't got the baby bouncer down from the loft yet, I didn't have anything to put Felix in while he napped.

'Amena, lovey, would you mind bringing the Moses basket down from my bedroom?'

'Yes, that's fine,' she said.

Thankfully, Felix didn't stir when I put him down so I was able to get on with quickly making a tuna pasta bake.

Just after 5 p.m., my mobile rang and I saw Louisa's name flash up on the screen.

'It's Mummy,' I called to Edie. 'Do you want to come and say hello?'

Edie ran in as I accepted the call and handed her the phone.

'Hi, Mumma,' she said.

I could hear Louisa chatting to her in the background and asking her about soft play and what we were doing.

'Nana's cooking tea and the baby's sleeping,' Edie told her. Then she handed me the phone.

'Was Edie joking about the baby?' laughed Louisa. 'Did she mean her dolly?'

'No, she's right,' I replied. 'We've had a new arrival this afternoon.'

I trusted Louisa implicitly; she'd grown up around my fostering and understood how important it was to keep information about the children I fostered confidential. I told her that his name was Felix and he'd been abandoned.

'That's so sad,' she sighed. 'What would make someone do that?'

'I don't know, lovey, but that's what the police are trying to find out.'

I could tell that she felt guilty that Edie was staying over.

'Charlie and I don't have to stay at the hotel tonight,' she told me. 'We can get a cab back later after the evening reception.'

'No, you two enjoy having a night off,' I told her. 'We'll be fine. Edie loves the baby and he seems to be a contented little thing.'

As if on cue, Felix suddenly started stirring in the Moses basket and let out a loud cry.

'Oh, I think I'd better go,' I said. 'He's probably hungry.'

'OK, thanks, Maggie,' said Louisa. 'We'll be there as early as we can in the morning.'

'There's honestly no rush,' I told her.

She and Charlie both worked and didn't get much time alone together so I really wanted them to enjoy their evening.

I warmed up a bottle for Felix and he gulped it down, his blue eyes focused intently on my face.

'I bet you're wondering who on earth I am, aren't you, little man?' I murmured as he drained the last dregs of milk. 'If only you could tell us where your mummy is.'

After I'd winded him and changed his nappy, it was time for me to dish up dinner.

The girls, Jordan and I sat around the table and tucked in. It had been several months since I'd eaten dinner one-handed with a baby on my knee and it was tricky to say the least. I thought back to the last baby I'd cared for, and I remembered it was a six-month-old called Annie who had come to me on a respite placement while her mum had taken her older brother into hospital for brain surgery.

After dinner, Amena cleared up while Jordan and Shola watched some TV and I took Edie upstairs for a bath.

I figured Jordan and Shola could skip their bath tonight just to make life a bit easier.

'Can the baby have a bath too?' Edie asked.

'I don't see why not,' I said. 'But Felix will have one after you.'

Due to safeguarding rules, unless children were siblings I would never bathe them together.

I got Edie in the bath first while I put Felix on a changing mat and took his clothes off. He was tiny, but his skin was velvety soft and pink.

'You're perfect, aren't you,' I cooed.

Once Edie was out and dry and in her pyjamas, I took Felix's nappy off and put him on a little baby seat in the bath.

I closely supervised while Edie very carefully and gently got a sponge and trickled water on him.

'Good girl,' I told her. 'You're doing a great job. He really likes that.'

'But he's not smiling, Nana,' she said.

'He hasn't learnt to smile yet because he's too little, but that will come in a few weeks,' I told her.

I could see Edie taking it all in.

Felix was starting to get cold and his little lips were quivering, so I quickly lifted him out, dried him and put him in a clean nappy and babygro.

Then we went to my bedroom where Edie was to sleep on a little fold-out bed. I read her a story on my bed, then it was time to settle her down. I could see she was tired after all that running round at soft play.

'Baby Felix go sleepy now too?' she asked hopefully.

'I need to give Felix another bottle and then he'll come to bed a little bit later on,' I told her.

I was keen to get Edie to bed first. I hoped if she was in a deep sleep, there was less chance of Felix waking her if he struggled to settle.

One down, four to go, I thought to myself as I headed downstairs.

After a cup of warm milk and a biscuit each for Shola and Jordan, I took them upstairs.

'No bath tonight,' I told them. 'Brush your teeth and get into your jammies, then you can both read for ten minutes before lights out.'

'OK,' they nodded.

I could see they were tired after a long week at school. While they took it in turns to use the bathroom, I lay Felix on one of the beds and did a quick tidy up of their room.

He looked around the room and suddenly seemed very alert and awake.

'Is it going to be a long night, Felix?' I cooed. 'Are you going to have me up all night?'

To be honest, sleepless nights didn't faze me as they were part and parcel of the job. I'd cared for children of all ages who hadn't previously had boundaries or proper bedtimes or even a proper bed to sleep in, so I was used to getting up and down in the night.

Once Shola and Jordan were tucked up in bed, I made Amena and I a cup of tea before she headed upstairs to her room to watch a film.

'I hope the baby doesn't cry and wake you up,' I told her.

'I'll be OK,' she said. 'You know me, I'm a heavy sleeper so I probably won't hear him. If it gets really bad, I'll put my earphones in.'

'Night-night, flower,' I smiled. 'Fingers crossed for a quiet night for all of us.'

I sat down and put the TV on. It was the local news and as I turned the volume up with the remote control, I just caught the end of an item.

'. . . a newborn baby boy abandoned at a railway station . . .'

Suddenly, photos flashed up on the screen showing a white rabbit and a familiar blue blanket.

My heart started racing and I looked down at Felix in my arms. *They were talking about him.*

There was a police inspector on the screen now speaking directly to the camera and making an appeal to the baby's mother.

'We are concerned for your welfare and I urge you to make contact either with the police, your local hospital or a GP's surgery. It's really important that we know that you are safe. I would also urge anyone who has information that could help us to reunite this baby with his mother to please come forward.'

I cuddled Felix tightly in my arms.

Poor little mite.

But my heart also went out to his mother. Abandoning your baby in a public place was an action of someone who was truly desperate.

My chest felt heavy with sadness as I gave Felix his bottle and changed his nappy before we headed upstairs to bed.

Thankfully Edie was fast asleep as I carried Felix into my bedroom. I'd set up the Moses basket next to my bed and I gently lay him in it. I placed the little white rabbit next to him and then tucked the soft blue blanket over him. I hoped the familiar smell of his mummy and his home would help to soothe him.

'There you go, sweetie,' I whispered. 'Night-night.'

Felix stared up at me with his big blue eyes.

What must he be thinking?

Finally, I got myself into bed. It had been a long day and suddenly I felt exhausted. However, as I lay there in the darkness, all I could think about was his mother.

Where was she? Was she lying somewhere thinking of her baby boy and wondering where he was?

I hoped that she had seen the police appeal and knew that he was safe and being well cared for.

And I hoped that, for Felix's sake, she was safe too and that we'd find her very soon.

THREE

Comings and Goings

To be honest, I was dreading that first night. I expected to be up and down with Felix as it was very normal for a baby to be unsettled, especially one as young as he was. He was in a strange place and he would be missing the familiar smell and voice of his mummy.

Newborn babies weren't known for being quiet and I was worried that his cries would wake up Edie and then the rest of the house.

However, much to my amazement, Felix had settled straight away and had only woken up three hours later at 3 a.m. I think I must have been on high alert because the minute I heard him stir, I'd leapt out of bed and picked him up. Edie had woken up briefly when she'd heard him crying but I'd quickly whisked him downstairs for a feed.

Felix had gulped his milk down. His eyes had started to close halfway through his bottle but his little lips had kept on sucking. By the time he'd finished his bottle he was fast asleep. He didn't even stir when I changed his nappy and then, holding my breath, I'd carefully lowered him back into the Moses basket.

Incredibly, I didn't hear another peep from him until just after 6.30 a.m. I wasn't used to broken nights and I was relieved it hadn't been the ordeal I'd been expecting.

I took Felix downstairs and made a cup of tea as I waited for his bottle to warm up.

Even though he must have been hungry, he didn't make a fuss. He just looked around the room.

'You're such a good boy,' I smiled.

He was so contented and alert. It was still dark outside and the lamp in the kitchen cast shadows on the wall that seemed to transfix him.

After he'd had his bottle, he lay peacefully on the sofa next to me while I drank my tea.

Just after half past seven, I heard Edie stir.

'Where are you, Nana?' she shouted from upstairs.

That was enough to wake Shola and Jordan up too and soon everyone except Amena was in the kitchen. She was a typical teenager and liked a lie-in at the weekend so I knew she wouldn't surface for some time yet.

'Can we make some pancakes?' asked Shola.

It had become a regular Saturday morning treat and I knew Edie loved them.

'Pancakes! Pancakes! Pancakes!' Edie chanted, jumping up and down.

'OK,' I said. 'But let me go and get Felix's Moses basket from upstairs so he's got somewhere safe to lie while I cook.'

It really was a juggle but I was thankful that he was such a good baby.

By 8 a.m., I felt like superwoman. All awake children were tucking into Nutella and banana pancakes and Felix was fast asleep again.

Half an hour later, there was a knock at the door. I was surprised to see Louisa and Charlie standing there.

'Wow, you're early,' I gasped.

'I felt so guilty about you having Edie to cope with as well as a newborn baby and all the other kids,' replied Louisa.

'Don't be daft,' I said. 'They've all been really good and Felix has been amazingly chilled out.'

I took them through to the kitchen where Edie ran towards her parents' outstretched arms.

'Nana's got a baby,' she told them excitedly.

'I know,' smiled Louisa. 'Where is he? I want a cuddle.'

'He's actually just nodded off,' I told her, leading her over to the Moses basket.

'He's really cute,' she sighed, stroking his hair. 'He's so tiny. How could anyone abandon him like that?' Louisa spoke in a low voice so Charlie and the other children wouldn't hear, as she knew that what I'd told her was to be kept confidential.

'I know,' I nodded. 'His poor mum must have been really desperate.'

Louisa was listed with my agency as my respite support, which meant she'd had training and gone through all the necessary checks. So I knew I could leave her to keep an eye on Felix and the other children downstairs while Charlie helped me get the baby stuff out of the loft.

'Thanks, lovey,' I told him as he carried the pram, a baby bouncer, a playmat and a few other things down the ladder from the hatch. I really appreciated his help as it was such a difficult job to do by myself.

'There you go, Maggie,' he smiled.

'That's great,' I said. 'I'm all set now.'

'How long's the baby going to be with you?' he asked.

'I don't honestly know,' I shrugged. 'We'll just have to wait and see what happens.'

I knew I was unlikely to get any updates from Social Services as it was the weekend. There was always a duty social worker who I could call if I had any problems, but Rupinder wouldn't be working so I probably wouldn't hear from her until Monday. I couldn't help wondering if there had been any new developments in tracing Felix's parents.

Louisa and Charlie stayed for a coffee then prepared to head home.

'Bye, flower,' I said, giving Edie a big hug.

She ran over to the Moses basket.

'Bye-bye, baby,' she said, patting Felix on the head.

'Careful, Edie,' warned Louisa. 'Nice and gentle.'

He started to squirm and cry.

'Sorry, Maggie,' said Louisa apologetically.

'Don't worry,' I reassured her. 'He's due another bottle now anyway.'

The rest of the weekend carried on in much the same vein. I knew a five-week-old baby was never going to get into a routine but I wanted to keep things as simple as possible for my own sanity and also for Felix.

Even newborn babies could experience trauma – research shows that trauma can start in the womb as the baby is able to pick up on its mother's stress levels. Although Felix was only small, he would still register that everything around him had changed. The way I held him in my arms and even gave him his bottle was probably different to how his mum had done it, and he would know my voice and smell wasn't the same. It would take him time to get used to his new world.

The only thing we did was to nip out to the supermarket on Saturday afternoon so I could stock up on some more nappies and a few essentials.

Shola and Jordan loved coming shopping with me and we always made it into a bit of a game. I'd tell them an item on my list and they'd find it for me and put it in the trolley.

'Can I have a magazine?' begged Shola when we were in the part of the shop that sold the newspapers and magazines.

'Yes, flower, if you want to buy it out of your pocket money,' I told her.

I glanced at all the newspapers laid out on the shelf and one of the headlines caught my eye – POLICE SEARCH FOR MUM OF NEWBORN LEFT AT STATION.

Seeing it there in black and white on the front of a national newspaper that thousands of people would read really shook me.

Jordan must have seen me looking.

'That's like the blanket the baby's got,' he said, pointing to the photo of the blue elephant blanket that was identical to the one currently tucked over Felix in his car seat.

'Oh, yes, you're right,' I smiled.

Thankfully he was too young to understand that Felix *was* the abandoned baby.

I thought about Felix's mum and wondered if she had seen any of the appeals and if she had come forward. Perhaps it had been a spur-of-the-moment decision and twenty-four hours without her baby had made her realise the enormity of what she'd done?

However, even if she did decide that she'd made a terrible mistake and she wanted him back, would the police and Social Services allow it after she'd abandoned him in such a – as the newspapers were describing it – 'callous way'?

On Sunday, my friend Vicky had kindly invited us all round for lunch. I'd called her the day before and told her about the baby.

Vicky was a fellow foster carer so she just 'got it', although over the past year she'd been through a really tough time. Like me, she'd been a single foster carer for over twenty years although we worked for different agencies. She'd been fostering a group of three brothers – six-year-old Grant, John, ten, and Robert, thirteen. Their biological parents were both alcoholics and they'd witnessed domestic violence at home. When they'd first gone to live with her, they'd shown some really challenging behaviour but Vicky had refused to give up on them. Slowly, they'd started to calm down and Vicky had formed a really strong bond with them. So much so, that she'd made the decision to take them on full-time. She was even about to apply for a Special Guardianship Order, which meant there would be no more Social Services involvement and she would have full parental responsibility for all of the boys until they reached eighteen.

But then one day Robert had told one of his teachers that Vicky had lost her temper with him and slapped him. As with any allegation made by a child, Social Services had to treat it seriously and do a full investigation despite Vicky denying that it had ever happened.

The boys had been removed from her care and had gone to live with another carer and, heartbreakingly, Vicky had never seen them again.

It was the most horrific thing to go through and it had been deeply distressing to see my friend so broken. The police had said there were no criminal charges for her to answer but it had taken Social Services months to carry out their investigations. Until the investigations were completed, Vicky wasn't allowed to foster any other children so she'd lost all of her income overnight. She'd managed to keep her head above water with a loan from a family member and she found work in a supermarket to help make ends meet. Six months ago, Social Services had finally come back to say all of the allegations were unsubstantiated and Vicky was cleared. However, she'd been so traumatised by the whole experience that she hadn't fostered since.

She was still currently working in the supermarket while she made a decision about her future.

Vicky was such a compassionate person that I felt it was a huge loss to the fostering world if she didn't care for children anymore. But I knew how low she'd been and her mental health was the most important thing. I was looking forward to catching up with her over lunch.

'Hi,' smiled Vicky as she opened the door.

Shola and Jordan had been to Vicky's house several times so they ran straight through to the playroom where she still kept all of the toys that she'd used for her fostering.

'And this must be Felix,' she said, looking down at the car seat that I was carrying. 'He's gorgeous!'

'He's bloomin' heavy,' I smiled.

I carried him through to the kitchen. He'd nodded off in the car so I gently put him down and undid his cardigan and loosened the buckle on his seat so he didn't get too hot.

'Are you exhausted?' Vicky asked me as she put the kettle on.

'To be honest, he's not been that bad,' I told her. 'He wakes up every three or four hours for a feed but then he goes straight back to sleep.'

'That's great,' she said.

As Vicky was still a registered carer, I knew I could trust her to keep any information confidential so I'd told her how Felix had been abandoned.

'I can't believe he was left at a station,' she sighed. 'How awful. What must his poor mother have been going through? And I wonder if there's a dad around?'

'I know,' I said. 'I can't stop thinking about her.'

'Have they traced her yet?' asked Vicky.

'Not that I know of,' I replied. 'The police have been appealing for her to come forward but there's no word as yet. I just hope she's OK.'

Vicky nodded in agreement.

'Well, I've got some news,' she said, taking a sip of tea. 'I've been offered a little one to foster.'

'Oh, that's brilliant,' I smiled. 'I didn't know you'd decided to start fostering again.'

'I'm not sure I have,' she sighed. 'There are still so many hoops to jump through and I don't know whether I have the energy to put myself through it.'

She explained that her agency had asked her if she would be willing to take on a three-year-old girl.

'I won't know for sure until it goes to court in a couple of weeks whether it's even going to happen,' she shrugged. 'But I'm so nervous and I'm not sure I can do it.'

'How can you be nervous?' I asked. 'You've been doing this for over twenty years. You're one of the best foster carers that I know.'

I could see that everything Vicky had been through had taken its toll.

'I've lost confidence in myself,' she sighed. 'And it still hurts so much. I'm still questioning what went so wrong that Robert felt he had to make those allegations against me.'

Even though those allegations had been proven unsubstantiated, if Vicky decided she definitely wanted to foster again she would have to go in front of a panel. Her supervising social worker would write a report about the allegations and what the outcome was, and the panel would formerly dismiss it.

'I just don't know if I can face it,' she said.

'At least it would give you closure,' I suggested. 'Then you can properly draw a line under it.'

'But even though the allegations have been shown to be false, the panel could still make some recommendations,' Vicky told me. 'They might say I have to go for more training or reduce the number of children that I'm allowed to foster. I just don't know whether I can put myself through any more.'

I felt desperately sorry for her.

'If you don't want to go alone then I'd be happy to go with you,' I told her.

I wouldn't be allowed to sit in on the panel itself but I could wait outside and be there to support Vicky.

'That's kind of you but I just don't know if I want to do it,' she told me.

I understood. It had been awful to see my good friend go through such a hideous time and she'd really struggled.

'You have to do what you think is right for you,' I told her.

Fostering wasn't something that you could do half-heartedly. It was all-consuming, taking over your life, and Vicky had to be sure it was what she wanted.

'I'm so torn,' she said. 'But then I see kids like Felix and I think I've got so much to give them.'

'You certainly have,' I said, giving her a hug.

After Vicky's, we headed home for the afternoon. Amena was busy doing homework so I got on with some tidying while Shola and Jordan played and Felix napped. I'd forgotten how much babies his age slept and it gave me a window to get things done.

I was tidying up the kitchen when my mobile rang.

'Maria!' I said, surprised. 'How are you doing?'

Maria was Shola and Jordan's foster carer.

'I'm doing so much better, Maggie, thanks,' she said.

I'd only spoken to Maria a couple of times since her back operation and she had sounded rather weak and frail.

'You sound a lot brighter,' I told her.

'I really am,' she replied. 'So much so, I'm going to tell my supervising social worker that I'm happy to have Shola and Jordan back next week.'

It took me by surprise as it was sooner that I'd been expecting, but I knew they'd be pleased.

'That's wonderful,' I said. 'I'll go and get them so you can tell them yourself.'

'Yes, thanks, that would be lovely,' said Maria.

I went into the living room and held out my mobile.

'Maria's on the phone for you,' I told Shola and Jordan. 'Would you like to say hi?'

They both nodded eagerly so I put my mobile on speaker-phone so they could hear Maria.

'Hi, you two,' said Maria. 'I've missed you both so much. But guess what?'

'What?' asked Shola.

'My back has got lots better so you're only going to have a few more sleeps, then I'm coming to pick you up from Maggie's.'

I could see them both taking the news in.

'They're really pleased, Maria – I can see it in their faces,' I told her, putting the phone back to my ear.

'Thank you so much for having them,' she told me. 'Steve's spent the past few weeks looking after me so there was no way he'd have been able to look after them too.'

'It's been a pleasure,' I told her. 'They're great kids.'

They really were. A lot of carers didn't like doing respite care. They didn't like children constantly coming and going and preferred to be settled with a permanent set of children. However, I enjoyed it and I liked the variety. It was also more relaxed; there were no formal settling-in periods or notice or managed goodbyes. It was just one carer helping out another. I still had to keep daily recordings, but I didn't have to build up a relationship with their school or their birth parents or attend lots of meetings like their full-time carer did. Also, because I generally only did respite care for other carers who were from the same agency, the children placed with me tended to be children that I had met before or already had a relationship with.

After I'd put the phone down to Maria, I went and sat with Shola and Jordan.

'That's such lovely news,' I beamed. 'You must be so pleased to be going back to Maria and Steve.'

'We like it at your house too,' said Jordan.

'I know, but I bet you'll be glad to go home,' I said and they both nodded.

Tomorrow I'd mention it to Becky, my supervising social worker, and then Maria and Steve would probably come and collect the kids later in the week.

It was more change in the house. However, it meant that I could now focus more of my attention on baby Felix and all of the unanswered mysteries about his background. But the question was, were we ever going to get any answers?

FOUR

All Change

Monday morning brought the usual rush, but now there was the extra element of having a baby in the mix. Felix was up, changed and fed by the time Shola, Jordan and Amena came down for breakfast. The taxi came to take Shola and Jordan to school just after eight, leaving time for a quick chat with Amena over cereal and toast before she headed off to school.

'Shola and Jordan's foster carer, Maria, rang yesterday,' I told her. 'She's feeling a lot better so they're probably going to go back to her house later on this week.'

'Oh, that's really sad,' she sighed. 'Well, for us, I mean – not them. They're sweet kids.'

'They are,' I nodded. 'But they were always going to leave and it's nice for them that they can go home.'

As Amena ate her toast, I could see that she was deep in thought.

'What is it, flower?' I asked her.

'Don't you get really sad when kids leave?' she said.

'You know, Louisa used to ask me that a lot when she lived here,' I told her. 'She came to me when she was thirteen, so there were children coming and going all through her teenage years.'

It was always hard for me to say goodbye, but I had chosen this life and I knew it was part of the job. However, Louisa grew attached to a lot of the children and got upset when they left.

'I would tell her that it was good that she cared for them so much as it meant she had a big heart,' I said to Amena. 'And missing them was a natural emotion. But I would also tell her that we had to try to focus on the positives and be happy for them that they'd moved on to a new home.'

It was really hard but Louisa and I would always talk about the children who had lived in our home and we'd keep in touch with as many of them as we could.

When Shola and Jordan had first arrived, I'd explained to Amena that they were only staying temporarily. However, this didn't stop her from becoming attached to them and she had got used to them being around.

'Just because they're moving back home doesn't mean we won't see them again,' I told her. 'We can invite them round for tea.'

Even though they'd only been with us for a few weeks, their departure would take a bit of getting used to. The house would feel quiet without them.

'Anyway, we've still got the baby,' Amena smiled.

'We certainly have,' I told her, patting her hand. 'Felix will keep us both busy.'

I didn't have the heart to tell her that I didn't know how long we would have him for. It was all so unknown right now.

I was hoping to hear from Rupinder this morning to update me about what was happening and if there had been any word from the police.

After Amena left for school, I put Felix in the baby bouncer and started clearing up the breakfast things. A few minutes later, I noticed that he'd nodded off.

'Bless him,' I sighed.

He was almost starting to get himself into a routine and I noticed that he generally liked a sleep two hours after he'd woken up.

When my mobile rang, I quickly reached for it, keen not to disturb him.

'Hello,' I said quietly.

It was Rupinder.

'How is everything?' she asked. 'How's Felix been over the weekend?'

'He's been great,' I told her. 'He's such a good baby. He drinks all his bottles, he's pretty content and he sleeps.'

'That's great,' she replied.

There was one question that I was desperate to know the answer to.

'Have you heard from the police?' I asked her. 'Have they found his parents?'

'I've just got off the phone to the inspector actually,' Rupinder told me.

I held my breath.

'Unfortunately, there's no news. They had a few calls but they've all turned out to be hoaxes or time-wasters.'

It never failed to astound me that people thought it was OK to give the police false information.

'Oh, that's so frustrating,' I sighed.

I was hoping there would have been a few genuine leads after all the appeals on TV and in the newspapers.

We just had to carry on until we knew a bit more. Rupinder talked me through all of the usual things that I did when a new child came into my care.

'Please could your register him at your GP and then that means he can see a health visitor,' she told me.

'No problem,' I said. 'I can do that today.'

Babies as young as Felix had to have regular health visitor checks and weigh-ins, and he would soon have to start having his immunisations.

There was always plenty of admin and things to sort for the first few days after a new child arrived.

Later that morning, Becky phoned.

'How are things going?' she asked me.

I told her what we'd been up to and how there had unfortunately been no updates from Rupinder about Felix's mum.

'It's so sad,' she sighed. 'I saw it was on the news.'

'I spotted it on the front page of the papers too,' I replied.

She also told me that my fostering exemption had been approved so I now had permission to foster more than three children at any one time.

'It's ironic really as you're not going to need it,' she added. 'Shola and Jordan's social worker got in touch this morning to say they're going back this week.'

'Yep, that's right,' I said. 'Maria called me yesterday and told me.'

Even though I'd been expecting it, I was surprised when Becky said Maria wanted to collect them tomorrow after school.

'Is that manageable?' she asked.

'Well, it will be,' I replied. 'I'd better get their washing on though!'

We had known the children were going to be with me for at least a couple of weeks while Maria recovered so she'd sent them over with quite a lot of stuff.

When I finished my phone call with Becky, I carried Felix in his bouncer up to Shola and Jordan's room. Because they were ten and eight, they were allowed to share a room. Different gender siblings that were aged eleven or over weren't allowed to share rooms.

I pulled their cases out from under their beds. If I packed most of their stuff today, I could do the last few things with Shola and Jordan that evening.

But, as I started taking clothes out of drawers, Felix's eyes suddenly sprung open and he started to cry.

'It's OK,' I soothed.

I went downstairs and gave him a bottle and changed his nappy, but for some reason he just wouldn't settle.

'Now when I've got so much to do, you get all clingy,' I joked.

I spent the rest of the day jigging Felix in my arms, moving the bouncer with my foot or pacing up and down with him. I even put him in the pram and walked him round the block but nothing seemed to help him to settle.

By the early afternoon, I could see he was exhausted; his little eyes would start to close but then spring open a few seconds later and he'd start howling again.

All I could think was that he had a tummy ache or colic or perhaps he was missing his mummy? I had so much to do to get Shola and Jordan packed up and ready for the following day but no spare hands to do it with. It was at times like these that it was tough being a single carer. I'd got so used to doing it on my own over the years and I loved it, but there was the odd moment when I wished I had another adult there to help out.

When I heard a knock at the door, I realised that it was Shola and Jordan back from school. Even though Felix was still grizzling, I put him down in the Moses basket and went to let them in.

As they took off their coats and put down their bags, I told them the news.

'Guess what?' I said. 'I talked to my supervising social worker today and she told me that Maria and Steve are coming here after school tomorrow to collect you.'

'Wow,' replied Shola. 'What about our stuff?'

'I'll fix you a snack and then I'll help you both to do some packing,' I told her. 'I was hoping to make a start but Felix has been a bit unsettled today.'

'He looks OK now,' said Jordan as we went into the kitchen.

Lo and behold, while I'd been in the hallway talking to the children, Felix had finally given in to sleep.

'He must be exhausted,' I sighed. 'He hasn't napped since this morning.'

I didn't want to risk moving him now in case he woke up. Instead, I got the baby monitor and put it next to his basket while I went upstairs with Shola and Jordan.

Slowly but surely, we gathered their stuff together and filled up their cases.

Because it had been a respite placement and Shola and Jordan were always going to return to live with Maria and Steve, there were no drawn-out goodbyes. We all belonged to the same fostering agency, so I knew I'd see them again at the fun days and the Christmas and Easter parties that the agency organised.

However, goodbyes were important, especially for children who were moving on to adoption or going back to their birth parents, but I wasn't a fan of big emotional goodbyes for any child. Change was hard, particularly for children who were in the care system; to have a big fuss made, with people weeping and wailing and telling them how much they were going to miss them, wasn't beneficial for the child. It was nice to mark them leaving my house in some small way though.

'Amena will be back soon,' I told them. 'So let's have a special dinner together before you go home. What would you like?'

'Pizza!' yelled Shola and Jordan in unison.

'Pizza it is then,' I laughed.

I was happy with that as it would mean a night off from cooking for me.

When we went back downstairs, Felix was still fast asleep. I was reluctant to wake him as I knew how tired he must be, so I let him sleep on.

However, by the time Amena came back and we'd tucked into our pizza, he was wide awake and on my lap.

When I tucked Shola and Jordan into bed that night, he was in my arms.

'One more sleep, then tomorrow night you'll be in your own beds,' I told them.

'I'll be back in my own bedroom,' said Jordan.

'I bet you can't wait,' I smiled.

'But I'll miss baby Felix and Amena,' said Shola sadly.

'And they'll miss you too,' I told her. 'But you'll hopefully see them again soon.'

They could come round for dinner and if Maria had any follow-up hospital appointments, I was happy to help.

Soon I was regretting my decision to let Felix sleep on earlier. He was wide awake and despite giving him his usual bath and bottle, he still hadn't nodded off.

I was in bed by eleven, but he was kicking around in the Moses basket next to me.

'Bedtime now, sweet pea,' I soothed.

I thought turning out the light might help signal to him that it was sleep time, but as soon as I did he started to cry.

What followed was a very long night of me trying to get Felix to settle. I rubbed his back, massaged his tummy, sang to him, rocked him, paced the floor with him but he still refused to go to sleep. It was around 4 a.m. before he finally nodded off and I felt like a zombie when my alarm sounded just over two hours later.

Bleary-eyed, I got Shola and Jordan off to school.

'Are Maria and Steve still coming to get us later?' Jordan asked excitedly.

'Yes, lovey, they'll be here tonight after school to pick you up,' I told him.

Fuelled by coffee and chocolate, I managed to keep myself going for the rest of the day. Felix thankfully seemed fine and much more settled. I was just exhausted.

Before I knew it, Shola and Jordan were back from school. Then, five minutes later, Maria and Steve arrived at the door.

'Come in,' I smiled.

Maria was still a bit tender from her operation so the children had to be careful around her.

'Don't hug me too hard,' she laughed as Shola ran over to her.

While Shola and Jordan did a last sweep of their room to check they hadn't left anything behind, I made Maria and Steve a cup of tea.

They also met Felix.

'Aw, what a sweetheart,' sighed Maria. 'Talking of babies, how are Louisa and Edie?'

'She's not a baby anymore,' I smiled. 'She's three now.'

'Gosh, where does the time go?' replied Maria.

I told them how Edie was obsessed with Felix.

'Perhaps she'd like a little brother or sister?' Steve suggested.

'Maybe,' I smiled.

Louisa had always said she wanted two children but I didn't like to ask her if she was planning on getting pregnant again. It was such a personal decision and one that was none of my business, but I'm sure she and Charlie had had plenty of chats about it.

After we'd finished our tea, Steve loaded the children's cases into the car. He came back in clutching a big bunch of pink roses.

'Just to say thank you so much,' said Maria, giving me a hug.

'It's been my pleasure,' I told them. 'They're lovely kids.'

We went to get Shola and Jordan, who were watching TV with Amena in the living room.

'Come on then,' grinned Maria. 'It's time to go home!'

They jumped up and both gave Amena a big hug before giving me one too.

'Enjoy sleeping in your own beds,' I told them, ruffling their hair. 'See you soon.'

They both nodded and, without a second glance, ran out of the front door to the car. Amena stood with me on the doorstep as we waved them off.

'They look so happy,' she sighed.

'And so they should be,' I said, grabbing her hand and giving it a squeeze.

We watched and waved as their car disappeared off down the street. As I walked back up the front path, I heard my mobile ringing. I rushed into the house to answer it.

It was Rupinder.

'Maggie, I've got some news. The police have just this minute called me.'

She paused.

'They've found Felix's mum.'

It took me completely by surprise as yesterday there hadn't been any leads at all.

'Wow, how did they find her?' I asked.

Rupinder explained that a midwife had seen the appeals and recognised the blue blanket and the baby's name, and had contacted the police this morning.

'So the mum didn't give birth in secret then?' I asked, puzzled.

'No, not at all,' replied Rupinder. 'She had him at the local hospital and had been seen by midwives throughout her pregnancy.'

The midwife who had phoned the police worked in the community, and she'd been to visit Felix's mum a couple of times at home since she'd given birth.

'Is the mum OK?' I asked.

'The police said she is,' Rupinder told me. 'They're with her now at her flat, asking some questions.'

It was a huge relief.

'Listen, Maggie, the police are due to call me back once they've spoken to Felix's mum,' she told me. 'I should know a bit more then so why don't I pop round later and we can have a chat?'

'That would be great,' I said. 'What's her name?'

'I'm afraid I don't even know that,' Rupinder replied.

My head was spinning with so many questions about Felix's mum: why had she done it? Would the police charge her with child abandonment? Would she get Felix back? But my overwhelming emotion was relief that she was OK.

I couldn't resist picking up Felix and giving him a cuddle.

'We've found her,' I whispered, kissing the top of his head. 'We've found your mummy.'

FIVE

A Breakthrough

It was another couple of hours before Rupinder came round.

'Sorry it's so late,' she said, 'but I thought that I'd call round on my way home from the office.'

'No, it's fine,' I told her. 'I'm desperate to know more.'

'Well, I do have a bit more information from the police,' she told me.

I put Felix on a playmat on the floor while I made us both a cuppa. Amena was upstairs in her room.

'I'm just relieved that his mum's OK,' I told Rupinder. I voiced my worry that if you had been desperate enough to abandon your baby like that, you were going to be in a pretty bad state yourself.

'Yes, I had the same concerns as you,' replied Rupinder. 'But the police said she was fine. In fact, they described her as very calm and rational.'

She explained that Felix's mum was called Emily. She was thirty-six and worked as a financial adviser.

'Gosh, that really wasn't what I was expecting,' I said,

having imagined a teenage mum who hadn't dared tell her family that she was pregnant.

'What about the dad?' I asked.

'There isn't a father around,' replied Rupinder. 'Emily's a single mother. In fact, she chose to have a baby on her own.'

Things were getting more confusing by the minute.

'What do you mean?' I asked.

She explained that Emily had told the police that she'd always wanted to be a mother. But when she hadn't met anyone she wanted to have a baby with by the time she was in her mid-thirties, she'd decided to have IVF using donor sperm.

'Apparently she had two failed attempts and an early miscarriage before she finally got pregnant with Felix,' Rupinder told me. 'She spent over £10,000 trying to have a baby.'

It was all so strange. Why would someone who had wanted to be a mum so desperately and spent so much money on it then abandon their child? Not only that but leave them in a public place to be found by a stranger.

'It's so odd,' I sighed. 'Did she say why she'd abandoned Felix like that?'

Rupinder shrugged.

'She said she thought that she would be able to cope but, once he was born, she'd found it all too much and had decided she wasn't cut out to be a mum at all,' she continued.

'Apparently she was very calm and rational about it. She said she hadn't thought through the disruption a baby would cause to her life and realised that she couldn't do it on her own.'

It just didn't ring true to me.

'But why didn't she contact her GP or mention to the midwife that she was struggling?' I asked. 'Rather than taking him to the train station and leaving him there?'

'She apparently said that she'd made her mind up and she didn't want talking out of her decision,' replied Rupinder. 'She thought going through the official channels would take too long and she wanted Felix to find a new family quickly.'

None of it felt right.

'It sounds to me like she has the baby blues and this could be a kneejerk reaction to that?' I suggested. 'Maybe she just needs help and support?'

'Emily's refusing to entertain that idea and is insistent that she's not depressed,' Rupinder told me. 'She told the police that she had five weeks of it and realised that she's simply not cut out to be a mother.'

'Has she been checked over by a doctor?' I asked.

'She's refused point blank to see a GP or be checked over at A&E,' added Rupinder. 'Unless the police feel that she's in danger of seriously harming herself or anyone else then there's not a lot that they can do.'

They couldn't make her get checked over or talk to a health professional if she didn't consent to it.

The police had given Rupinder the details of the community midwife who had phoned in about Emily and she'd given her a call.

'I've arranged to see the midwife first thing in the morning,' she told me. 'I thought it might help us shed some light on what was going on in Emily's life.'

Although Felix's mum had been found, to me it didn't feel like we were any closer to knowing the truth.

'So what happens now?' I asked. 'Will the police charge her with child abandonment?'

'I'm not sure,' replied Rupinder. 'They've asked her to come to the police station so they can carry out a formal interview with her. Then it's up to them.'

I knew from past cases that the police would seek guidance from the Crown Prosecution Service (CPS) to see whether they should press charges.

I was also confused about what would happen with regards to Felix.

'Will Felix stay with me for now?' I asked.

Rupinder explained that Emily had consented to what was known as a Section 20, meaning she had given permission for Social Services to have parental responsibility for Felix.

'What if she changes her mind and decides that she wants him back?' I asked.

'It doesn't seem that way at the moment,' sighed Rupinder. 'She's adamant that she would like Felix to be adopted.'

'But that might change,' I replied.

'It might,' shrugged Rupinder. 'She's also saying that she doesn't want to have any contact with him at all.'

It all seemed so final.

'We'll start by trying to slow things down and encouraging her to see him,' said Rupinder. 'I think she needs to give herself time and Social Services need to make sure she understands the implications of any decision that she makes.'

If Emily did want Felix to be adopted, it would be a different team that would have to talk to her and start the process off.

'And what if she suddenly decides that she made a terrible mistake and wants Felix back?' I asked.

Surely someone couldn't abandon their baby and then just expect to be handed him back?

'After everything that has happened, she would have to go through a parenting assessment,' said Rupinder.

Suddenly Felix started to squirm and cry on his playmat.

'I'm coming, little man,' I said.

As I walked over and scooped him up in my arms, I noticed Rupinder glance at the clock on the wall.

'Yes, it's getting a bit late,' I nodded. 'I need to get some tea on for me and Amena.'

'Where are the other two little ones?' asked Rupinder.

'They've gone back to their foster parents,' I said sadly. 'They'd just left when you called actually.'

'The house must seem really quiet,' she said.

'Yes, I suppose it does,' I sighed.

With Felix in my arms, I walked Rupinder to the front door.

'You look completely baffled, Maggie,' she said to me as she hovered in the doorway.

'I am,' I said. 'I'm just confused by the entire situation.'

'At least his mum has been traced and we know who she is now,' she told me.

'Yes, that's true,' I said, ruffling Felix's hair. 'It's a relief to know that she's safe.'

'If you like, I can pop round in the morning after I've seen Emily's midwife?' Rupinder suggested.

'I'd really appreciate that,' I told her.

I was curious about what she would say and I was hoping that she could shed more light on things.

★

After Rupinder had left, I gave Felix a bottle then started making some pasta for tea.

Rupinder had been right: the dynamic of the house had changed and it suddenly seemed very quiet without Shola and Jordan there. Amena, like most teenagers, spent a lot of time in her room and I missed having the siblings around, chatting and playing.

You'll get used to it, I told myself.

It always took a few days to adjust and settle after children left.

After dinner, Vicky rang me.

'I've made a decision,' she told me. 'I'm going to start fostering again. I've told my social worker that I'll take on the three-year-old.'

'That's wonderful!' I said. 'I'm so pleased for you.'

It was a fairly quick process and she was due to go in front of the panel within the next few weeks.

'Do you want me to take you?' I asked her. 'I meant it, you know, when I said I was happy to come along for support.'

'That's really kind of you but I'm going to be brave and go on my own,' she told me.

I was so proud of Vicky. I knew she was scared but she wasn't letting her fear stop her from going back to doing what she loved.

'For what it's worth, I think you've made the right decision,' I told her. 'You're an amazing foster carer and that little girl is going to be so lucky to come into your care.'

'Thanks, Maggie,' sighed Vicky.

She'd been such a supportive friend to me over the years and I was glad that I had been able to be there for her at what I knew was the hardest time of her life.

Allegations were one of the most heartbreaking things for foster carers to deal with. The whole process was long and traumatic and I'd known a lot of foster carers who had resigned rather than put themselves through it.

'Onwards and upwards from now,' I told her. 'Hopefully you can finally draw a line under it and move on.'

'I hope so, I really do,' she said.

I didn't tell her about Felix's mum being found. For some reason, I didn't feel quite ready to share the news yet as I was still trying to get my own head around it.

My heart felt heavy with worry as I put Felix to bed that night. I felt anxiety about his mum as well as concern for Vicky. I just wished I could ensure that everything went smoothly for her. I desperately hoped her new placement with the little girl would give her a renewed faith in the job and she could get back to doing what she did best – transforming children's lives with love, patience and understanding.

The following day, Felix and I had a quiet morning at home. I was keen to see Rupinder when she came round and I wanted to know if the midwife had shed any light on Felix's mum.

She arrived just after eleven.

'Did you manage to speak to the midwife?' I asked.

'I did,' she nodded. 'She was a really lovely woman.'

Rupinder talked me through their conversation. The midwife had visited Emily at her flat for the first three weeks after Felix was born.

'She thought she was managing brilliantly for a first-time mum, especially as she'd had a long and difficult birth,' Rupinder told me.

Emily had been in labour for nearly two days. Felix's heart rate had dipped so they thought they were going to have to do a C-section but, in a last-ditch attempt, they'd managed to get him out with forceps.

'The midwife said that Emily was always showered and dressed with make-up on when she visited, and the flat was immaculate. She'd even been baking apparently.'

She also said that Emily had seemed very organised, and had made long lists about when Felix had fed and for how long and when he'd had a dirty nappy.

Rupinder said the midwife had had no concerns at all.

'Both mum and baby seemed happy to her and doing really well,' she shrugged.

Emily had been discharged from the birth team and transferred to the care of the health visitor.

'Had the health visitor seen her?' I asked.

'No, not yet,' replied Rupinder. 'Emily was due to see the health visitor last week but she hadn't been in the couple of times that they called.'

I was intrigued about what outside help and support Emily had had and why no one else had come forward sooner about the baby.

'Has she got any family or friends around her?' I asked. 'I'm surprised no one else recognised Felix when he was in the media.'

'Apparently not,' Rupinder told me. 'Emily's from New Zealand.'

She'd told the police that her mum had died a couple of years ago and she had one sister, Anna, who was still in New Zealand.

'The police have passed on her sister's number to me so I'm going to give her a call, but according to Emily she's about to have her own baby in the next few weeks, which is why she hasn't been able to come over to the UK to see her.'

Rupinder explained that she'd sent Anna an email asking her when would be a good time to talk, as New Zealand was thirteen hours ahead of the UK. She'd also got the details of Emily's work from the police.

'It's like a jigsaw puzzle,' she sighed. 'It's a case of putting all of the pieces together to try to get a full picture of Emily's life.'

I firmly believed we needed to get a better understanding of what was happening because, as things stood, I certainly didn't feel that we were getting the full picture.

Over the next few days, Rupinder did her best to find out as much as she could about Emily and her life. She called me with regular updates.

The following day she had a call from Anna in New Zealand.

'She'd spoken to the police and understandably she was really upset,' she told me. 'She's really shocked about what's happened – very distressed and tearful on the phone.'

'Did she have any idea Emily was struggling?' I asked.

Rupinder shook her head.

'Absolutely no clue,' she shrugged. 'She told me how Emily had been so happy to be having a baby. She'd gone back to New Zealand for a holiday when she was six months pregnant and Anna said she'd been full of excitement about having a baby.'

She'd called Anna when Felix had been born and sent her regular updates.

'They'd video-called each other a couple of times a week for the first few weeks and she said that Emily seemed to be doing OK,' Rupinder added. 'She said she seemed tired as Felix was feeding all the time and she was worried as his weight had dropped below his birth weight at one point, but she said Emily had been reassured by the midwife that this was normal.'

Anna told Rupinder that her sister had never been diagnosed with depression or had any mental health issues as far as she knew.

'She's as baffled as we are,' Rupinder shrugged. 'She feels really helpless and she's clearly worried about her sister, but obviously as she's about to have a baby it's impossible for her to fly over to the UK.'

'Has she spoken to Emily herself?' I asked.

'No,' replied Rupinder. 'That was what was upsetting her the most. Ever since the police contacted her she's been trying to get in touch with Emily. She's called multiple times a day and emailed too, but Emily hasn't got back to her.'

All Rupinder had been able to do was reassure her that Social Services and the police were in touch with Emily and were trying to understand what had happened and decide what was best for her and Felix.

They sounded like a close family and I couldn't imagine how upset and helpless her sister must be feeling with the imminent birth of her own baby to cope with too.

'The poor woman,' I sighed. 'She must be going out of her mind with worry.'

It was all so baffling and bizarre. What on earth had happened to make Emily go from an excited mum-to-be to someone who was prepared to leave their newborn on a train station platform?

SIX

First Meetings

Over the next few days, Rupinder carried on trying to gather as much information as she could about Emily and Felix. She'd called at her flat to see how she was and to give her an update on the baby.

'It was so strange,' Rupinder told me. 'She clearly didn't want me to come in so we just talked on the doorstep. It was obvious that she couldn't wait to get rid of me.'

Rupinder described how she'd seen a large pile of things bundled up in the hall by the front door.

'There were lots of bin bags and I could see a boxed-up steriliser, a baby monitor and a crib,' she said.

'I asked Emily what it all was and she said it was some things that she needed to take to the charity shop,' she added. 'It was all of Felix's baby stuff, Maggie. She was obviously getting rid of the lot and it was all practically brand-new.'

Was it a sign that Emily really didn't want him back or was it that she couldn't bear to have a reminder of him in the flat?

'She didn't ask me a single thing about Felix,' Rupinder continued. 'She was very polite but very evasive around anything to do with the baby. It's like she's just not interested.'

Rupinder also told me that the police had been in touch with Emily's work.

'They chatted to her boss and one of her colleagues,' Rupinder told me. 'They were completely shocked by what had happened. They said Emily had been really excited about the baby.'

They'd explained that Emily had been in touch with them to tell them Felix had been born and they had sent her some flowers and a card but they hadn't heard anything from her since then.

There was also the issue of contact. Rupinder had raised it a few times but Emily was still adamant that she didn't want to see Felix. With a baby as young as he was, contact could be four or five days a week and up to four hours at a time. Social Services were keen for Emily to have as much of a relationship with Felix as she could in case he ever went back to live with her. Babies changed so quickly and it was important for her to be around him.

'I explained that even if adoption is eventually what she decides, it's really important for Felix when he's older to have a few photos of them together,' said Rupinder. 'So he knows what his birth mum looked like. Contact is one place that we could do that. I explained it might also help her to make a decision.'

'You can't make her do it if she's not keen,' I said.

The local authority had a duty and a responsibility to offer contact to birth parents. They had to evidence that they'd made it as easy as possible for them to make contact and that they'd offered multiple opportunities.

Despite this, some birth parents choose not to come to contact whereas others would do anything not to miss it. I had one mum who was so desperate not to miss contact with her child that she discharged herself early from hospital and came straight to the contact centre.

A few days passed and Rupinder called me again.

'You're not going to believe this, but Emily's changed her mind,' she told me. 'She's agreed to contact.'

Rupinder had managed to find space in a contact centre for the following day. It was all very last minute but I was pleased. Suddenly, I had a glimmer of hope. It may have taken time but as soon as Emily saw Felix, she might fall back in love with him and remember what she was missing.

That morning, I felt strangely on edge as I got Felix ready. I wasn't sure what to expect or how Emily was going to react when she saw him.

I'd arranged to meet Rupinder at the contact centre half an hour before Emily was due to join us. I liked to get there early and get settled before the birth parents arrived. It also meant that I could make myself scarce before they got there.

Contact was being held at a centre that I'd been to several times before over the years – it was a seventies brick building tagged onto the side of a Social Services office. It was very basic and a little tatty and run-down, but it had a big car park at the front so I knew I'd always get a space.

I lifted Felix out of the car in his car seat and carried him up the steps to the white PVC door at the front. There was no sense that Emily was going to run off with Felix or harm him, so this was a contact centre that was used for parents who were low-risk and who didn't pose a threat of absconding with their child. There were a couple of security guards who worked between the contact centre and the neighbouring Social Services building. Sadly, social workers were often threatened by clients, so there needed to be a security presence at all times for their protection.

As I pushed open the door, I saw Rupinder waiting in the reception area.

'Hi,' she said. 'How are you doing?'

'OK,' I said. 'I feel a little bit nervous actually – I'm not sure how this is going to go.'

'Me neither,' replied Rupinder. 'I'm not sure how keen Emily actually is to see Felix but she said she's coming and I'm glad that she's giving it a try.'

Even though I was apprehensive, I was also intrigued to meet Emily. I hoped it would somehow give me a greater understanding of how she'd got to this point and also an insight into her state of mind.

As I looked around, I realised the centre had been given a bit of a spruce-up since I'd last been there several months before. The faded carpet had been replaced with wood-effect laminate flooring and the walls had been given a lick of yellow paint. It still didn't look very cosy though – the windows had those fabric strip blinds that you find in offices and there were hard plastic chairs instead of the comfy sofas that were provided in some centres. All along one wall were big storage cupboards that were full of toys suitable for children of different ages.

In the contact room there was a big red padded mat in the middle of the floor with a few baby toys set out on it.

'I know Felix is a bit young for toys but I thought it would give Emily something to do if she was struggling,' Rupinder explained.

'Shall I make sure that I'm out of the way before she arrives?' I asked her.

Some birth parents didn't want to meet the person who was fostering their child and I never knew whether I was going to face hostility or even aggression. I was often viewed, like Social Services, as 'the enemy'. I was seen as one of the baddies who had taken away their children and therefore it could feel very uncomfortable being around some birth parents. Other parents desperately wanted to know and meet the person who was looking after their child.

'I think it might be nice for you to be here so that you can answer any questions that Emily might have,' Rupinder told me. 'She doesn't strike me as someone who's going to be hostile but if things do get uncomfortable, you can always go and wait in the office but let's see.'

'I'm happy with that,' I replied.

Wherever possible, I liked to meet birth parents and work with them and share information about their child. For children who were older than Felix, it was good for them to see there was no animosity between their parents and their foster carer.

While Rupinder lingered around reception, I took Felix into the contact room. I got him out of his car seat and lay him down on the playmat.

I was pleased that he was awake as some babies slept through contact, which was often frustrating for birth parents.

'Mummy's coming to see you,' I told him, stroking his cheek. 'That'll be nice, won't it?'

I really hoped that it would bring Emily some comfort to see him and be around him. A few minutes later, Rupinder poked her head into the room.

'She's here,' she told me in a low voice.

I felt ripples of apprehension in my stomach as I got up off the floor. I nervously smoothed my hair and brushed down my black trousers.

I lingered in the doorway of the contact room as a woman walked into the reception area.

'Hi, Emily,' smiled Rupinder. 'I'm glad you found it OK.'

Emily looked immaculate. Her chestnut brown hair was glossy and poker-straight, and she was wearing a navy blazer, striped top and jeans.

'This is Maggie,' Rupinder told her, turning to face me. 'She's the foster carer who's been looking after Felix.'

I swallowed the lump in my throat as they walked towards me.

'Nice to meet you,' said Emily, holding out her hand and shaking mine in a businesslike manner.

Although she was fully made-up, close up I could see that she looked tired and gaunt and her grey eyes had a blankness about them.

'Hi, how are you?' I asked.

'I'm really well, thank you,' she replied, giving me a weak smile.

'And here's Felix,' said Rupinder, gesturing into the contact room. 'He's having a bit of a kick around on a playmat at the moment.'

At the mention of Felix's name, I could almost feel Emily bristle and she suddenly looked away.

'Would you like Maggie to sit with us as well?' Rupinder asked her. 'I thought it might be useful if you wanted to ask her any questions about Felix or pass on any information to her about his routine or what he likes.'

'Yes, if she wants to that's fine,' Emily replied blankly.

As Emily walked in, she went straight past Felix and sat on one of the plastic chairs over at the far side of the room. She hadn't acknowledged him at all or even looked at him.

'It's such a lovely day, isn't it?' she said, gazing out of the window next to her. 'I went for a run this morning and I think I'll go and get my nails done this afternoon.

'I'd really like to go on holiday,' she continued. 'If I go into town, I might go into a travel agents and see if they've got any last-minute deals. I'm thinking about Majorca – have either of you ever been there?'

'No, I haven't, I'm afraid,' I replied.

Rupinder and I swapped looks while Emily talked about holidays and buying new clothes and tidying her flat. She hardly paused for breath as she spoke about anything and everything except Felix. It was all very odd.

Perhaps it was nerves? I knew that contact could be very stressful.

She was here to see and spend time with her baby and I knew I needed to try to help her engage with him and encourage some interaction between them. I went over to the playmat and picked Felix up. Then I went and sat back down on a chair next to Emily. While she might not be holding him, at least that way she could see him.

'Felix, here's Mummy,' I said. 'Say hi to Mummy.'

Emily continued to stare out of the window rather than look at her son.

'He's such a good baby. He loves his bottle and most of the time he sleeps really well. He loves his playmat too,' I smiled. 'He's starting to make noises now when he's lying there.'

'Oh, that's nice,' replied Emily blankly.

She tucked a strand of hair behind her ear and I noticed that her hands were shaking.

'I think I might go to Marbella,' she sighed. 'I've heard it's really lovely there.'

It was just bizarre. Maybe I had to be more obvious in my attempt to get her to engage with her son?

'Emily, would you like to hold Felix?' I asked her. 'I'm sure he'd love a cuddle with his mummy.'

'Oh, no, thank you,' she said firmly but politely. 'Not at the moment. He seems quite happy with you and I don't want to disturb him.'

Whenever Rupinder or I tried to steer the conversation towards Felix, Emily would avoid the subject. I also noticed she still hadn't even looked at him and now I had him in my lap, she avoided my gaze.

'Maggie, how did Felix get on when you saw the health visitor?' Rupinder asked me.

She already knew the answer but was obviously trying to engage Emily.

'She was really pleased with him,' I told her. 'She said he'd put on three pounds so he'd clearly been well looked-after. She also said he'll need to start having his injections soon.'

I turned to Emily, who was now fiddling with a ring on one of her fingers.

'Has he had any injections?' I asked her.

'Who?' she replied, looking confused.

'Felix – did you take him for his first lot of jabs?'

Emily shrugged. 'No, I don't think I did,' she said vaguely.

Felix suddenly started squirming and flexing in my lap. I looked at my watch.

'I think he's probably due a bottle,' I said.

'Emily, would you like to feed him?' Rupinder asked her. She suddenly looked flustered.

'No, I don't think so,' she said. 'I've got to go to the toilet.' She suddenly got up and left the room.

Rupinder and I looked at each other.

'She's behaving so oddly,' I whispered.

'It all must be very strange for her,' she replied.

Rupinder went to the kitchen to warm up Felix's bottle while I paced the room with him so he didn't get upset.

'Don't worry, little man, your milk is coming,' I soothed.

It was Emily who came back into the room first. She didn't say anything but returned to the chair on the other side of the room. She was wringing her hands and shifting around in her seat. She looked anxious and I could tell something wasn't right.

'Are you OK, Emily?' I asked her, going to sit back down beside her.

She turned round and leant towards me, and I could see a look of complete panic in her eyes.

'Are those cameras?' she whispered, gesturing to the ceiling in the corner of the room.

'Yes, they're CCTV cameras,' I told her. 'They're all over the centre just for security but they're nothing for you to worry about.'

I could see Emily was getting really flustered and she was visibly shaking now.

She suddenly jumped up.

'I'm sorry,' she said. 'I can't do this. I've got to go.'

And, before I could stop her, she ran out of the contact room and out of the front entrance.

SEVEN

Moving On

Rupinder came dashing back into the room with a panicked look on her face.

'Was that Emily leaving?' she gasped. 'What's happened? Why did she go?'

'I honestly don't know. She asked me about the CCTV cameras, then she just went into a panic and got up and ran off,' I told her. 'It was all very strange.'

'I'd better go and find her and check that she's OK,' replied Rupinder.

She ran out to the car park to look for Emily while I stayed in the contact room with Felix. He was getting more and more fractious by the second and I knew he wanted his bottle.

Rupinder came back a couple of minutes later.

'There's no sign of her,' she panted. 'Her car's gone. I've tried calling her and it just goes straight to voicemail.'

'Do you think we should be worried?' I asked her.

'I'm sure she just had a wobble,' replied Rupinder. 'I'll keep trying to get hold of her and I'll go round to her flat to see her if necessary.'

I was left in a state of complete and utter confusion. I'd done many contact sessions in my time but this had been one of the most bizarre.

'It was all so odd,' said Rupinder, as if reading my mind.

'It was like Felix wasn't here,' I sighed. 'Emily didn't interact with him or want to go anywhere near him. She wouldn't even look at him.'

Thankfully at his age, he was too young to register that.

'No matter what, she came here today,' said Rupinder. 'And that's progress. I think we need to try again.'

I nodded.

'Perhaps it was the contact centre that was making her feel on edge?' I suggested. 'She really didn't like the cameras.'

I appreciated that coming to a contact centre to see their children was hard for birth parents and it was a stressful experience. It wasn't a natural, relaxed environment; it was a sterile, unfamiliar place and I could understand why parents felt like they were being watched and judged.

As I put Felix over my shoulder to wind him, I could see Rupinder mulling it over.

'I don't know what you think about this, Maggie,' she said, 'but I don't feel that Emily is a threat to Felix. So what do you think of the idea of having the next contact session at your house? Perhaps in a more relaxed environment, she might open up and take more of an interest in Felix?'

I thought it was a great idea.

'That's absolutely fine by me,' I nodded.

'I'd come along too,' Rupinder reassured me. 'And I would offer to go and collect Emily and take her there so your address wouldn't be too obvious.'

Over the years, I'd often done contact sessions at my house. I much preferred it to taking babies and children to contact centres. It was a lot more laid back and comfortable, and it would also be more relaxing for Felix to be in a familiar environment. It could only happen in situations where the birth parents were no threat to the child and there had been no aggression shown towards me or the social worker. Due to safeguarding rules, it would also have to be during the daytime when I had no other foster children there.

I left the contact centre that morning feeling a little more hopeful. Driving home, I mulled it all over in my mind. Today hadn't been great but Emily had turned up and maybe the next session at my house would be more successful?

It was all about little steps, and regular contact was so important with babies because they developed so quickly. It was about getting to know Emily too and hopefully she would start to open up about the situation and her worries about being a mum.

The minute I walked in the door, my phone beeped with a message.

It was Rupinder.

Got hold of Emily. She's OK. She wouldn't talk about why she'd left but I said I'd catch up with her tomorrow so don't worry. See you at the LAC review.

It was a relief to know that she was OK.

'Hopefully Mummy will see you again soon, Felix,' I cooed as I lifted him out of his car seat. 'And next time, she might give you a cuddle.'

I really hoped that would be the case.

In a few days, we were due to have a Looked After Child (LAC) review. It was a meeting at which everyone involved in Felix's care gathered to discuss where we were at and what the plan was going forward. LAC reviews were useful as they tended to give everyone some clarity and ensure that we were all on the same page. Emily and Felix's situation had been so strange and confusing that I wasn't sure we were going to get that much-needed clarity, but it would be good to talk things over.

Emily would be invited to attend, and Rupinder would be there with my supervising social worker, Becky, perhaps a GP or health visitor and maybe someone from the police. It would be chaired by an Independent Reviewing Officer, or an IRO as they were known. An IRO was someone who was independent from everyone else involved in the case, and their role was to look at the whole picture and make sure that every decision made was in the child's best interests and that their needs were paramount.

Rupinder got in touch a couple of days later.

'Emily's just emailed to say she won't be coming to the LAC review,' she told me.

My heart sank. That wasn't a good sign.

'So my manager has asked how you'd feel about holding it at your house?' she added.

'Absolutely,' I replied. 'That works well for me.'

Again, like holding contact at my house, it was a much more convenient option, especially with a young baby like Felix. Having a discussion in my living room rather than in a meeting room at Social Services helped make things feel a lot more relaxed.

The LAC review was looming but I also had something else on my mind. Vicky was due to go in front of the panel to talk about the allegations that had been made against her and hopefully draw a line under them so she could start fostering again.

The panel would be held at her fostering agency and there was normally around seven people sat round a table in a meeting room. It would be led by a panel chair and other people in attendance could be social workers, former foster carers or even young people who had grown up in the care system. Every local authority and fostering agency had to have a panel. It was the same group of people that approved foster carers but also deregistered them if their behaviour hadn't been deemed acceptable.

I knew Vicky was increasingly worried about it; as the date drew closer, she'd become more and more anxious.

'I've hardly slept the past few nights,' she told me when I rang up on the morning of her panel to wish her luck. 'I'm terrified, Maggie.'

'It will be fine,' I tried to reassure her. 'They'll be on your side.'

'I hope so,' she sighed. 'I don't think I can take any more.'

I'd offered again to go with her to the panel and wait outside but she assured me that she'd be OK on her own. However, I couldn't get her out of my mind all day and I was wondering how it had gone.

That afternoon, there was a knock at my door.

'Coming!' I yelled.

I assumed it was Amena back from school and being too lazy to look in her bag for her key. But when I opened it, Vicky was stood there.

She collapsed into my arms sobbing and my heart sank.

'Oh no,' I gasped. 'What happened? You've been on my mind all day. Was it awful?'

'No, it was fine,' she sniffed.

'Oh, thank goodness!' I sighed. 'You had me worried there.'

'Sorry,' she smiled, wiping away her tears. 'I'm just so relieved.'

Vicky came in and I gave her some tissues and made her a cup of tea. Slowly, she calmed down and started to explain what had happened. The panel had talked through the allegations and the outcome, but Vicky said they'd mainly wanted to know how she was feeling and if she'd had enough support.

'They were just so lovely to me and I wasn't expecting that,' she sighed, her eyes filling with tears again. 'They were so concerned about me and what I'd been through, and they said they had absolute confidence in me as a foster carer.'

After the panel, Vicky's supervising social worker had taken her out for lunch and given her a bunch of flowers for her commitment to fostering.

I could see the sheer relief on her face.

'I finally feel like I can start to put this whole nightmare behind me and move on,' she said.

'Oh, I'm so pleased,' I told her. 'You deserve it after everything you've been through.'

She explained that in a few days, the three-year-old girl she would be fostering was due to arrive. It was the fresh start that she so desperately needed.

'Sorry, Maggie, I've just been banging on about me,' laughed Vicky. 'What's happening with you?'

I explained that I had Felix's LAC review the following day.

'It'll be fine,' I told her. 'Sadly birth mum's not coming but I'm looking forward to hopefully getting more of a plan in place.'

The following morning, things couldn't have been better timed as Felix nodded off half an hour before everyone was due. It gave me a chance to do a quick tidy of the kitchen and the living room. I put some biscuits on a plate and got the mugs out on a tray so I could offer everyone a hot drink when they arrived.

Rupinder arrived first with Felix's IRO, followed by Becky. It was the first time I'd met Peter, the IRO, who'd only been appointed a couple of days before. I guessed he was in his early fifties; he had a grey ponytail and was dressed casually in a jumper and jeans.

He introduced himself to me.

'I've been a social worker for twenty years and a manager for the past five,' he told me, giving my hand a firm shake. 'And I believe birth mum's not coming today?'

'No, sadly not,' I said. 'Felix is having a nap at the moment but hopefully you'll get a chance to see him before you go.'

As everyone else arrived and got settled in the living room, I went to sort out the drinks.

'I'll give you a hand, Maggie,' said Becky.

Felix was still fast asleep in the kitchen in his Moses basket with the baby monitor next to him. Becky hadn't seen him before so she tiptoed over for a little peek.

'Oh, he's lovely,' she sighed.

'He really is,' I smiled.

Once everyone had got their tea and coffee, Peter started things off.

'There's no one coming from the police today,' he said, looking at his notes. 'But I believe they're still deciding whether to press any charges against Emily, Felix's birth mother.'

'That's right,' nodded Rupinder.

The only other person there was the health visitor whom I'd taken Felix to see a couple of times.

'So, what's the situation with birth mum?' asked Peter. 'Because, reading the case notes, I'm baffled.'

I looked across at Rupinder.

'We're still trying to ascertain where she's actually at,' said Rupinder. 'We haven't really got a clear picture yet.'

She explained what had happened with Emily so far – how she'd told the police and Social Services that she'd decided that she no longer wanted to be a mum. How she'd refused contact at first and then when she had come along, she'd not interacted with Felix at all.

'It's very bizarre,' agreed Peter. 'And how's her mental health? Has she been assessed by anyone or checked by a GP?'

'She's refused point-blank so far,' replied Rupinder. 'She insists that she's fine.'

Marie, the health visitor, talked about how Felix was continuing to gain weight.

'Maggie says that he's sleeping well and loves his bottles,' she added.

'He certainly does,' I smiled.

Then Peter turned to me.

'How did you find Emily when you met her, Maggie?'

'I just found the whole contact session really strange,' I told him. 'Emily was talking about holidays and going jogging and getting her nails done – anything but the baby.

She didn't ask any questions about him – she wouldn't even look at him.'

'She's insistent that she wants him to be adopted but it just doesn't seem to make sense given all that she went through to have him,' Rupinder said.

'Do you think she's serious?' asked Peter.

'Who knows?' replied Rupinder. 'That's what Emily keeps saying and there'll come a time when we'll have to start believing her.'

He nodded.

'What do you think, Maggie?' he asked.

'I think there's something else at play here,' I said. 'Even though she's saying she's decided she doesn't want to be a mum, it doesn't ring true to me.'

Peter explained that we had to be guided by what Emily was saying.

'We need to keep talking to her and offering her the chance to see Felix, and explain that we can give her help and support if she needs it,' he said. 'But if, after all that, she's still insistent that adoption is the way forward, then we have to listen to her.'

He explained that if she did change her mind and wanted to keep Felix, she would have to have a parenting assessment.

'We can't just hand a baby back to someone who abandoned him like that,' he said. 'I'm just thankful that he was found so quickly.'

'It could have been a very different ending if no one had noticed the bag at the end of the platform,' nodded Rupinder.

'It's all very confusing,' Peter agreed. 'But for Felix's sake, I think we need to start parallel planning.'

This meant that Rupinder would make contact with the adoption team and give them information about Felix. From there, they'd allocate him an adoption social worker who would start looking through profiles of prospective parents on their books.

'I think it's important that we keep trying to engage Emily as much as possible,' nodded Peter.

'Maggie has agreed to have the next contact session here at her house,' added Rupinder. 'So we're hoping that will help Emily feel more comfortable than at the contact centre, so she might be more likely to interact with Felix.'

By the end of the meeting, it felt like we'd come to some kind of conclusion.

'It seems that parallel planning is the best way forward,' said Peter. 'We'll keep assessing Emily and keep communicating with her and encouraging her to see Felix. At the same time, we can't delay this baby's future so we'll go down the adoption route. So if Mum does decide this is her genuine wish, we will have already started the process and won't have wasted valuable time.'

Everyone was in agreement that this was the best way to proceed.

As they got their things together, the baby monitor suddenly sprung into life. A loud cry echoed through the front room.

'That will be Felix,' I smiled.

I went to get him from the kitchen and brought him into the living room. He blinked, his eyes wide with surprise, at all the new faces suddenly staring at him.

'He's a smasher,' smiled Peter.

'Would you like a hold?' I asked him.

'Oh, I'm OK,' he replied. 'I don't have any children of my own so I'm always a bit nervous around babies.'

I saw everyone else out while Becky stayed behind for a chat. She cuddled Felix while I made us another coffee.

'So how are you feeling?' she asked me as she bounced Felix gently on her knee.

'Confused,' I sighed. 'And frustrated. I want to help Emily but I don't know how.'

'You can't help someone who doesn't want to be helped,' shrugged Becky. 'Maybe she reached rock bottom and what she needs is time and sleep?' she suggested. 'As you know, Maggie, I've got two small children and if you're not getting any sleep, you can't think straight.'

'That's true,' I said.

I'd worked with enough mums to know that having a newborn baby was hard. It was particularly hard if you were doing it all on your own like Emily had been.

'You just go into survival mode during those first few weeks,' nodded Becky. 'It's relentless.'

'You're right,' I replied. 'But Felix has been with me for over a week so surely she would be feeling slightly better by now? And, even if you're exhausted, you'd still have an interest in your baby, wouldn't you?'

The support was there if Emily needed it, but if she didn't verbalise it then how could anyone help her?

'There's something going on that I can't put my finger on,' I sighed.

'Do you think she's got the baby blues?' asked Becky.

'It seems different somehow,' I shrugged.

I looked down at Felix sitting on Becky's lap.

'You want to see Mummy, don't you, Felix?' I smiled, stroking his cheek.

His mouth opened and he gave me a big toothless grin.

'Oh, did you see that?' I gasped. 'He just smiled.'

That was his first one.

'You clever boy,' I told him, which led to another grin.

Becky and I laughed but I also felt a deep sadness. It should have been Emily here seeing this. I wanted to pick up the phone and tell her all of the things that she was missing. All those 'firsts' that she wouldn't see if Felix wasn't with her. Is that what she truly wanted?

EIGHT

Last Chances

The voice on the other end of the phone was hysterical.

'Vicky, it's OK,' I urged her. 'Take a deep breath and tell me what's wrong.'

All I could hear was sobbing.

'It's Paige,' she said, her voice shaking. 'She's hurt herself.'

I tried to stay calm.

'How?' I asked. 'What exactly has she done?'

Paige was the three-year-old girl Vicky was fostering. She'd come into the care system a couple of weeks ago as her parents were alcoholics and neighbours had told the police she was regularly being left on her own. It was the first child Vicky had fostered in over a year since the allegations had been made against her, and I could tell that she was panicking.

'We went to soft play and she fell over in the car park on the way back to the car,' she wept.

'Is she badly hurt?' I asked.

'She's cut her knees and got gravel in her hands,' she sobbed. 'What am I going to do, Maggie? They'll think I've hurt her.'

It sounded minor to me but, after Vicky's experiences, I could understand why she was fearing the worst.

'Is Paige OK?' I asked her.

'She was crying at first when she saw the blood,' she explained. 'But I've bathed her knees and her hands and put antiseptic cream on them and plasters and she seems OK now.'

'Vicky, it sounds like you've handled it perfectly,' I told her. 'You've done all you can.'

'But what if they don't believe me when I tell them what happened?' she asked. 'What if they take her off me?'

It was clear that Vicky was catastrophising.

'If you're worried about it, then ring it in to your agency and report what happened as well as recording it in your notes,' I replied. 'Describe how it happened, where it happened and how you dealt with it and what you did to comfort Paige. And don't forget to do a body map drawing as well.'

This was an outline of a body that you marked with a cross where the child had hurt themselves. I reminded her to send it all in to her agency and Social Services that day, so if someone saw the cuts and bruises on Paige then Vicky would have already notified them about it.

After all her years of fostering experience, Vicky knew all of this but I could tell that she was upset and not thinking straight.

'Small children are always falling over and scraping their hands and knees,' I told her. 'Social Services are aware of that.'

'I know I'm overreacting,' she sighed. 'It's just after everything that's happened, I'm so scared of doing anything wrong.'

'You're a brilliant foster carer,' I soothed. 'You've been through so much, it's understandable that you're questioning everything but you've got to learn to trust your judgement again.'

'I feel so stupid,' she sighed again, but I completely understood.

I'd worked with some carers who'd had allegations against them and had ended up with Post Traumatic Stress Disorder (PTSD) after everything they'd been through. Having a false allegation made against you was something that every foster carer lived in fear of and it had been such a traumatic and stressful experience for poor Vicky.

'Ring me any time you need to if it helps,' I told her.

'Thanks, Maggie,' she replied. 'I really appreciate your support.'

Thankfully, talking things through had calmed Vicky down and I hoped she would start to settle back into her role and have faith in her abilities again.

A few days had passed since the LAC review and I realised that I hadn't heard any more from Rupinder about having the contact sessions at my house.

I messaged her to ask.

I'm struggling to get hold of Emily, she replied.

It was another couple of days before she called me back.

'I've found out why I couldn't get hold of Emily,' she told me. 'She was on a mini-break.'

'A mini-break?' I gasped. 'You're not serious?'

Of all the times for someone to choose to go away, now didn't seem like the most appropriate and I was astounded.

'Who did she go with?' I asked.

'Just on her own,' replied Rupinder. 'She said she had to get away.'

I honestly couldn't believe what I was hearing.

'I told her about contact but she was insistent that she didn't want to see Felix,' added Rupinder. 'I explained that it would be at your house this time and not at the contact centre but even that didn't persuade her. She just kept saying how adoption was the best thing for him and could I arrange for her to sign the papers?'

'How did you leave it with her?' I asked.

'I told her that if she did feel adoption was the best option, the last thing that she could do for her son was to have a couple of photos taken with him for his life-story book, then at some point in the future, when he's older, he'll know who his "tummy mummy" was.'

For every child who came into the care system, social workers and foster carers put together a book for them to look at when they were older. Sometimes, if they were adopted when they were little, they wouldn't have any memories of who had fostered them, where they had lived and how long they were there for. When they were older, a social worker would do what they called life-story work with them and they'd talk about why they had come into the care system and who they had lived with.

Personally, I liked to make memory boxes for the children who came into my care. For babies, I might save one of their babygros, their favourite toy, their first shoes and lots of photographs of them. It was so important for children in care to have that information.

'I explained that we'd need to do it this week and she said that she'd think about it,' Rupinder told me. 'I've got a meeting with the adoption team in a couple of days and I'll ask them to contact Emily.'

It was all so baffling and sad. I couldn't get a measure of Emily or what was happening with her, and she didn't seem prepared to reach out to Social Services for the support she might need to be able to keep Felix. It seemed like she was intent on having him adopted and nothing was going to change her mind.

It was another few days before I heard back from Rupinder.

'Emily's agreed to one contact session at your house tomorrow morning,' she told me. 'It's on the proviso that it's the last one and she's only coming to say goodbye to Felix and enable a couple of photos to be taken.'

'OK,' I sighed. 'If that's what she wants.'

As agreed, Rupinder was going to pick Emily up at her flat and bring her to my house. I suggested around eleven as I hoped Felix would have had his mid-morning nap and would be awake by then.

'I've said it will be for an hour but I think that's being optimistic,' said Rupinder.

The following morning, everything was ready. The house was clean and tidy, Amena was at school, Felix had had a good sleep and he'd just had a bottle.

I still refused to give up hope that Emily would start to reconnect with him. He was over two months old now and he'd changed so much in the past few weeks. His eyes were focusing on things more and he was making lots of babbling noises.

But my hope was mingled with doubt. Part of me wondered if Emily was even going to be there when Rupinder went to collect her. But, just after 10.30 a.m., my phone beeped with a text.

We're on our way. See you in 20 minutes.

I didn't want to answer the door to Emily with Felix in my arms in case it was too overwhelming for her. So I lay him on his playmat and put a few toys around him, including the fluffy rabbit that he'd been found with at the train station.

When the knock at the door finally came, I leapt up to answer it.

'Hi, Emily,' I smiled. 'Come on in.'

Emily was as smartly dressed and fully made-up as she was the last time. However, there was a blankness in her eyes, her hair was all matted and it didn't even look like it had been brushed.

'Would you like a coffee?' I asked.

'Oh, yes, please,' replied Rupinder.

Emily didn't say a word as I led them through to the kitchen. As before, she walked straight past Felix and didn't even look at him. She went and sat on the sofa.

'You probably heard Felix before you saw him,' I said. 'He's making so many noises now and is chattering away.'

Emily stared out of the patio doors into the garden. As I put the kettle on, I noticed her lean over and touch the radiator.

'Oh, are you cold?' I asked her. 'I can put the heating on if you'd like?'

'No!' she snapped. 'Don't do that.'

Rupinder and I looked at each other.

'I mean, no, thank you, I'm fine,' she said.

Emily seemed so anxious and on edge. She sat on the sofa in silence, wringing her hands.

The tension in the room was suddenly broken by the sound of Rupinder's mobile ringing.

'Sorry, I need to take this,' she said, jumping up. 'I'll go into the front room.'

Emily and I sat there in silence.

'As you can probably see, Felix has got his rabbit with him,' I smiled. 'I always make sure he has it in his Moses basket at night.'

'Oh, yes,' replied Emily vaguely.

I wasn't sure that she was even registering what I was saying.

'Why's that here?' she suddenly asked me, pointing at the baby monitor.

'What, the baby monitor?' I replied. 'Felix sometimes falls asleep in his bouncer or in his Moses basket and if I'm upstairs or in the living room doing jobs then it means I can still listen out for him and make sure he's OK.'

I didn't know what else to say but Emily looked absolutely terrified.

Then Felix suddenly started to cry. I didn't go to him straight away as I was hoping Emily might do it, but she just looked over at me with a scared expression on her face.

'He probably wants a nappy change,' I said.

I put the change mat out on the floor, picked Felix up and lay him down on it.

'Damn, the nappies are upstairs,' I said. 'I'll quickly run up and get one.'

I went upstairs to my bedroom and grabbed one from the cupboard, then came back down again. I walked back into the kitchen to find Emily kneeling on the floor with Felix on the change mat. She'd taken all his clothes off and he was completely naked. When she saw me, she jumped up.

'It's OK,' I smiled. 'You can change his nappy if you want, you're his mummy.'

'No, no,' she said, shaking her head. 'You do it.'

I was puzzled as to why she'd taken all his clothes off, but it was the first time I'd seen her interact with her son and I was secretly delighted.

'Had his nappy leaked through?' I asked her.

'No,' she said vaguely.

Emily quickly edged her way back to the sofa while I carried on changing Felix's nappy.

She kept gazing around the room as if she was looking for something and she seemed really agitated. I noticed she kept staring at the baby monitor.

'Are you OK, Emily?' I asked her. 'Can I get you anything?'

'No,' she replied, shaking her head.

Her behaviour was bizarre but I put it down to nerves. I was disappointed, as I had hoped that having the contact session at my house would help Emily to feel a bit more relaxed and less under pressure.

Once I'd changed Felix and got him dressed, I put him back on his playmat and carried on making the coffees.

'Rupinder must still be on the phone,' I told Emily. 'I'll just quickly take her a coffee.'

Emily was still staring out of the window but she nodded.

In the living room, I could see Rupinder was still on her call. I carefully put her drink down next to her on a side table and she gave me a thumbs-up.

'Sorry, I'll just be another few minutes,' she whispered and I nodded.

Seconds later, I walked out into the hallway just in time to see the front door slam.

My heart sank.

Emily.

She must have gone. She had run off just like she had done at the last contact session.

I ran into the kitchen to check on Felix.

He wasn't lying on the playmat anymore and he wasn't in his bouncer or in the Moses basket.

My heart started pounding in my chest.

I quickly bolted upstairs and checked my room, the bathroom and all of the other bedrooms.

But the utter dread in the pit of stomach told me what I already knew: Felix had gone.

And Emily had taken him.

NINE

On the Run

I'd never moved so fast in my life. I flew out of the front door and bolted down the path. I was certainly no runner and it didn't help that I was wearing slippers.

Thankfully, a few hundred yards in front of me, I could see Emily and what I hoped was Felix in her arms.

I didn't want to shout or scream as I didn't want to scare her and then have her run off again. I knew I needed to keep her calm, talk to her, and try to persuade her to come back to the house with me.

She was striding along at a fair pace. I took a deep breath and started to jog down the pavement towards her.

Please let me catch her, I willed as I pushed my body to carry on.

A minute later, I managed to catch up with her.

'Emily,' I puffed, gently tapping her on the shoulder. 'Emily, it's Maggie.'

She spun round. Thankfully Felix seemed fine and was looking around contentedly in her arms.

'Emily, where are you going?' I panted. 'It's really chilly out here and Felix will be getting cold. Why don't you come back to the house and I'll make you a nice cup of tea?'

Emily stared at me blankly. There was something so vacant about her; it was like she wasn't truly there.

'I'm really sorry,' she said. 'I'm afraid I can't.'

Her voice was robotic and devoid of any expression.

'Please, Emily,' I begged. 'Even if you don't want to stay, let's go back and talk to Rupinder and she can give you a lift home.'

I suddenly felt water drip onto my head and I realised that it was starting to rain. Panic was rising up inside me although I knew I had to appear calm.

'Emily, please come back to the house now,' I told her. 'It's starting to rain and you and Felix are going to get soaked.'

'No,' she said, shaking her head. 'I can't. I have to go somewhere.'

I wasn't sure where this was heading but I had to keep her talking. My mind was quickly assessing the situation as she spoke, wondering what the heck I could do.

Rupinder was probably still on her call in the living room, oblivious to the situation that was unfolding out here. Annoyingly my mobile was still lying on the table in the hallway so I felt helpless.

'Emily, I need you and Felix to come back inside with me,' I told her. 'We can talk about whatever's bothering you there.'

'Felix is getting really wet,' I added. 'We need him to be safe, don't we, and it's not good for a little baby to be out in the rain.'

'That's why I'm doing this,' nodded Emily. 'So Felix can be safe.'

Hearing her words made me feel really uneasy.

'Doing what, Emily?' I asked. 'What will make Felix safe?'

'I need to go down to the railway station and lie on the tracks with him and then we'll be safe,' she said. 'I didn't do it last time, but this time I need to get it done otherwise they're going to come for us.'

She was so matter of fact about it but I couldn't believe what I was hearing. I also knew I had to stay calm and not let Emily see my shock.

'Who's "they"?' I asked her.

Emily looked around her as if she was checking to see who was there. Then she leant towards me.

'The voices. The ones in the radiator and the baby monitor. They're always watching me,' she whispered. 'They know everything I'm doing. They were watching me at that centre the other day and I know they've put a bug in Felix's clothes. I couldn't find it when I searched him earlier but I know it's there. They've got them everywhere.'

Suddenly her face changed and she edged away from me.

'Hang on, do you work for them?' she asked. 'Are you bugged too? Or are you and that other woman actors?'

I really didn't want her to run so I knew my only option was to keep her calm and reassure her I wasn't one of 'them', whoever they were.

'Emily, I promise you that I'm not bugged and I don't have a camera,' I told her. 'I'm not one of them and I'm certainly no actor. I'm here to help you and Felix and keep you safe, and I promise you that I'm not going to hurt you.'

She burst into tears.

'No one can keep him safe. No one except me. They said they're coming for us so I have to take him with me,' she whispered, her eyes wide with terror. 'I thought if I left him then it would keep him safe but they said this is the only way.'

I swallowed the lump in my throat. How had we not realised that she was so ill?

'But how do you know that they're going to hurt you, Emily?' I asked her.

'I heard messages coming from the baby monitor and the radiator,' she told me matter-of-factly. 'And coming out of the TV at my flat.'

Fear prickled the back of my neck. There was something very, very wrong here and I had to do whatever I could to stop it.

'Bye, Maggie,' she said suddenly. 'I have to take Felix to the station now.'

Emily spun round to go but instinct made me reach out and grab on to her arm.

She looked shocked.

I knew I had to stay calm. I didn't want to spook her into running away with Felix.

'I know,' I said. 'Let's go back inside and talk to Rupinder. The train station's a long way from here and I'm sure she could give you a lift? We could ask her if she's heard the voices too?'

Emily suddenly looked terrified and stepped away from me.

'But what if she's working for them?' she gabbled. 'She'll tell them where we are and they'll come for us.'

Her whole body was shaking and I could see that she was genuinely terrified.

'It's OK, Emily,' I told her. 'I know you're frightened, but Rupinder doesn't work for them. She wants to help keep you safe just like I do.'

Suddenly Felix started to wriggle and cry in Emily's arms. The rain was coming down heavily now.

'It's so cold and wet and you can't take Felix to the train station without his blanket or his fleecy suit,' I told her. 'Why don't you come back to the house and get them? Then I can take you both to the train station?'

Emily looked like she was mulling it over.

'OK,' she nodded. 'You're right. Felix needs his blanket.'

'That's good,' I said, giving her a fake smile. 'That sounds like a plan.'

I didn't have a clue what I was doing but I knew I needed to get her back to my house and somehow let Rupinder know what was happening. My main priority was getting Felix off Emily in case she decided to run again.

'Why don't I hold the baby?' I suggested. 'You look so tired, Emily.'

She nodded.

'I'm so, so tired,' she told me. 'It feels like I haven't slept in months; I've been so busy writing my notes and my plan.'

'You poor thing,' I said. 'Let me carry Felix. I honestly don't mind. He must be getting really heavy.'

I held my breath as she mulled it over.

'It's OK,' she said. 'I'll keep hold of him for now.'

My stomach lurched. I had to think of another way to get Felix back safely in my arms and away from Emily. I couldn't risk him getting hurt.

Slowly we walked back up the street and up the front path. Rupinder was standing in the doorway.

'There you are!' she said. 'I just came off the phone and was wondering where everyone had gone.'

'Oh, we just went for a little walk didn't we, Emily?'

'Mm,' she nodded, still clearly suspicious of Rupinder.

I saw my mobile phone on the hallway table and I discreetly grabbed it and slid it into my pocket.

Looking at our wet hair and the expression on my face, Rupinder could clearly tell there was something wrong. She'd also noticed the fact that Emily was holding Felix.

'Is everything OK, Maggie?' she asked me.

'Yes, it's all fine,' I nodded, knowing the panic in my eyes told her a different story. 'Emily and I are going to get Felix's blanket from the kitchen then we'll come back and have a chat.'

As I followed Emily, I turned round to Rupinder and tapped my phone. Hopefully she would understand that I was going to message her. I just had to pick my moment because I knew how paranoid Emily was and, if she saw me texting, she might run off again.

In the kitchen, I found Felix's elephant blanket in his Moses basket and his fleecy suit.

'Here's his suit,' I told Emily. 'Do you want to put him in it?'

'OK,' she nodded.

She lay him on the sofa and knelt on the floor so she could get him into his suit.

While her back was turned, I quickly got my mobile out of my pocket and typed Rupinder a text.

HELP!! Call 999. E having breakdown. She wants me to take her to train station so she can lie on the tracks with Felix. Hearing voices and paranoid. I will take her in car and pretend to go to station. Text when amb here.

My hands were trembling, as I struggled to type the message as fast as I could. Thankfully Emily hadn't noticed as she was still fighting to get a wriggly Felix into his fleecy suit.

'Are you OK there?' I asked her. 'Do you need a hand?'

'No, I'll do it,' she snapped.

When Felix was finally ready, she grabbed the blanket from me and wrapped him in it.

'Quickly, we need to go,' she told me, looking around anxiously as if she was being watched. 'We have to get out of here or they'll come for us.'

Rupinder was waiting in the hallway. I could tell by the horrified look on her face that she'd read my message.

'Rupinder, I'm just going to drop Emily and Felix somewhere,' I said.

'OK,' she nodded. 'I'll wait here, Maggie.'

'Thank you,' I said. 'I've got my phone.'

I was having to think on my feet and, as far as I could see, this was the only way of doing things. I now knew there was no way Emily was going to hand over Felix willingly to either of us as she didn't trust anyone at this stage. My main priority was to make sure that he was safe.

I felt sick with nerves. I knew all that I could do now was kill time and drive around until Rupinder messaged me that she'd got help.

We walked to my car that was parked on the road outside the house. Emily insisted on putting Felix into his car seat in the back. Once she'd done that, she crouched down on the ground near the passenger door.

'Emily, what are you doing?' I asked her.

'Checking for bugs,' she said, running her hand along the underside of the car. 'They're always listening, you know.'

Finally, she got into the car.

'Please can we go?' she asked firmly. 'We need to get to the station as quickly as we can before they come for us.'

I took a deep breath and turned the keys in the ignition, hoping Emily didn't see that my hands were shaking.

She sat in the front passenger seat, shifting and looking around anxiously.

I felt so sorry for her. Again, I wondered how we had not noticed that she was clearly so ill? How had we let it get this far?

'The station's quite a long way from my house,' I warned her. 'It might take me a while to remember where it is.' I hoped and prayed that Emily didn't know this part of town and didn't realise that I was driving around trying to kill time.

'Please hurry up,' she begged me. 'Felix and I need to get there. We have to do it this time. It's the only way for us to be safe.'

I drove around as many back streets as I could, hoping that it would confuse Emily. I could see that Felix had fallen asleep in his car seat and I was grateful that he was oblivious to what was going on.

Every time we had to stop and wait at a junction, I was so thankful for the delay.

It felt like a lifetime had gone by before I felt my phone vibrate in my pocket. When we stopped at the next set of traffic lights, I looked over at Emily. She was staring out of the window, paranoid and clearly terrified.

Seizing the moment, I quickly pulled my phone out and glanced down at the screen at the message from Rupinder.

Help here. Head back.

My body sagged with relief. However, I knew it wasn't over yet. I couldn't relax until I knew Felix was safe – and Emily too.

As I drove back to my house, I did my best to take a different route, hoping that Emily wouldn't notice that we were nowhere near the station.

'Will we be there soon?' she asked me anxiously, wringing her hands.

'Just a few more minutes,' I lied.

As I drove back up my street, I felt my heart pounding in my chest as I saw the ambulance parked up outside of my house. When we'd got into the car, I'd deliberately locked the doors just in case Emily tried to jump out.

As I edged closer, I could see the front door was open and Rupinder and two paramedics were standing on the front path.

'What?' gasped Emily suddenly. 'Why are we back here?'

She turned to me with a horrified look on her face.

'Why did you lie to me?' she said, tears filling her eyes. 'They're going to come for us now. I knew you were in on it.'

Before I replied, I flicked the button to unlock the car doors. Within seconds, Rupinder pulled open the back passenger door, released the seatbelt and whisked Felix off the back seat.

'Nooo!' screamed Emily. 'Don't take him!'

She tried to clamber into the back seat but Rupinder quickly slammed the car door shut.

The paramedics walked towards the passenger door of the car.

'Maggie, help me,' Emily whimpered.

'I'm so sorry, Emily,' I sighed. 'I *am* helping you.'

She quickly pushed open the car door and tried to run off but thankfully the paramedics managed to restrain her. She let out the most heart-wrenching scream I'd ever heard as they bundled her into the back of the ambulance.

I felt sick and so, so guilty.

'Maggie, come into the house,' Rupinder called from the doorstep.

I ran up the front path while the paramedics battled with a howling Emily in the back of the ambulance. She was kicking and screaming and lashing out at them.

'Come inside,' Rupinder told me. 'You don't need to see this.'

Felix was on the hallway floor, thankfully still fast asleep in his car seat.

'She was going to kill herself and him,' I burst out. 'She's been hearing voices telling her to lie down in front of a train otherwise something was going to happen to her and Felix.'

'She's clearly very unwell,' nodded Rupinder. 'It could have ended so differently.'

I felt devastated for both of them. Deep down, I'd hoped that there would be some way that they could be reunited. But now Emily was clearly so unwell, those hopes were quickly fading.

I collapsed onto the floor at the bottom of the stairs, unable to believe what had just happened.

TEN

A Waiting Game

As we watched the ambulance pull away, I put my head in my hands and burst into tears.

'Oh, Maggie,' gasped Rupinder, closing the front door and rushing over to me. 'Are you alright?'

Once the tears started to flow, I couldn't do anything to stop them. All the intense stress and anxiety of the past hour came tumbling out.

'I've never been in a situation like that before and I was just so scared,' I sobbed. 'I was making it up as I went along.'

I hadn't known what to do for the best or how Emily was going to react.

'I was so worried that Emily was going to run off with Felix and that they were both going to come to harm,' I sniffed.

'Maggie, you did the best you could in that moment,' Rupinder reassured me. 'Whatever happens from here on, you kept them both safe. They're OK and Emily's hopefully going to get the help that she desperately needs.'

I got up from the bottom of the stairs and we went through

to the kitchen. Rupinder carried Felix in his car seat as he was still fast asleep, then kindly made me a cup of tea.

I blew my nose and tried to compose myself.

'I'm really sorry,' I told her. 'I'm not normally a crier.'

'It's OK,' she smiled. 'It's understandable after everything that's happened. You're probably in shock.'

When I'd finally calmed down, Rupinder asked if I'd mind talking her through what had happened so she could take some notes for her own records.

'I know it's hard going over it again but then at least I'll know everything so I can report back to my manager,' she told me.

'No, it's fine,' I told her. 'Honestly I'm feeling OK now.'

I explained how, when Rupinder had gone to take her call, Emily had seemed even more anxious and on edge.

'Her behaviour was really odd,' I said. 'She was asking me about the baby monitor and touching the radiator. And when I came downstairs from getting a clean nappy, she'd completely undressed Felix.'

I then told her what had happened when I'd taken the coffee to her in the living room.

'When I came back out into the hallway, I realised that she'd gone and so had Felix,' I continued. 'I was so scared.'

I described how, in a panic, I'd run down the street after her.

'It was only then that she told me what was happening.'

I explained that Emily said she had been hearing voices and thought people were talking to her through the baby monitor and the radiators, and the TV in her flat.

'She thought Felix was bugged and that people were watching her,' I added.

'And what were the voices saying to her?' asked Rupinder.

'She said they were telling her that she had to take Felix to the train station and lie on the tracks with him and only then would they be safe,' I continued. 'She said she hadn't been able to do it the first time so she'd left Felix at the station in the hope that if she wasn't with him then somehow he would be OK.'

'Oh, that's awful,' sighed Rupinder. 'But it makes sense why she didn't want to see him or go near him.'

'I still can't believe that Emily is so unwell and we didn't realise,' I replied, feeling my eyes fill with fresh tears. 'How did we not notice that she was suffering delusions and hearing voices?'

'She did a good job of hiding it,' nodded Rupinder. 'We both suspected that she was depressed and she was certainly acting oddly but she refused to see a doctor so there was nothing that we could do. All of this has been going on inside her head and she was obviously very frightened.'

All of Emily's bizarre behaviour over the past few weeks suddenly made sense.

'I feel so sorry for her,' I sighed. 'What will happen now?'

Rupinder explained that the paramedics would take her to A&E, where she'd be assessed by a psychiatrist.

'If, like you say, she was threatening to harm herself and Felix and is suffering from delusions and paranoia, they'll probably section her,' she added.

'Poor woman,' I said, shaking my head.

'Please don't beat yourself up about it, Maggie,' Rupinder told me, patting my hand. 'You did the right thing.'

I looked at Felix, who was thankfully still fast asleep in his car seat, oblivious to the drama that had been unfolding around him.

'I'll write up my report of what happened and if you could record it in your notes too, that would be useful,' Rupinder told me.

'Of course,' I nodded. 'And will you let me know what they say at the hospital?'

'Yes, I'll keep you updated,' she replied.

I could see a slight shake to her hands, too, and I knew she was trying to keep me calm while thinking through the next steps. She probably needed to get back to the office to report this immediately.

'Are you sure you're OK now, Maggie?' she asked.

'Honestly, I'm fine,' I said, knowing she needed to get off. 'I was just a bit shaken up after what happened. I'm fine now,' I said again to reassure her.

After Rupinder left, I felt totally and utterly exhausted so I decided that Felix and I were going to have a quiet day at home.

It was mid-afternoon before I heard anything more from Rupinder.

'The hospital has just called,' she told me. 'Emily's been sectioned and taken to a psychiatric ward.'

Although it was what we'd expected, I still felt incredibly sad. I had so many questions about what was going to happen now but I knew I had to be patient.

The following morning, Rupinder got back in touch.

'As there's no immediate family around, the psychiatrist who's treating Emily has agreed to have a chat to me,' she told me. 'I thought it might be useful for you to be there too. She might be able to tell us if Emily is well enough to see

Felix and we can ask if you can bring him up to the hospital at some point too,' she added.

'That would be good,' I said.

Rupinder had also agreed to update Emily's sister in New Zealand, who now had a week-old daughter.

'As you would imagine, she's desperately worried,' she told me.

'I bet she is,' I sighed.

We all were.

I knew when I went up to the hospital, I needed to be able to concentrate and listen to what the psychiatrist was saying, so I thought it was best not to take Felix with me. I didn't want to have to worry about him needing a bottle or a nappy change or becoming unsettled and starting to cry.

I knew Louisa would be at work, so I turned to the other person that I could always count on in a crisis: Vicky.

I called her and explained what had happened with Emily.

'That's awful,' she gasped. 'His poor mum. I'll happily come and look after him at your house if that works?'

'That would be great,' I said. 'Obviously all of his stuff is here and I'll make sure there are some toys out for Paige.' I hadn't met the little girl that Vicky was looking after yet, but after all my years in fostering I knew what three-year-olds enjoyed playing with.

Thankfully, things were going well for Vicky after her panicked call about Paige falling over.

The following morning, Vicky was there bright and early with a shy, red-headed girl clinging to her leg.

I knelt down so I was at her level.

'Hi, Paige,' I said gently. "I'm Vicky's friend, Maggie. It's lovely to meet you. Have you come to help look after baby Felix?'

She nodded.

'He's having a nap at the minute,' I told Vicky, and pointed out some juice and biscuits for Paige and also where Felix's bottle was.

'The nappies, wipes and change mat are over there,' I said, pointing to the corner of the room. 'When he wakes up, he might like to go on his playmat or he likes sitting in his bouncer.'

'Don't worry, he'll be fine,' Vicky told me.

'I know,' I smiled. 'I don't know why I'm telling you all this as you've looked after hundreds of babies.'

I was surprised at how nervous I felt. I suppose I was anxious about what the psychiatrist was going to say and it was the first time I'd left Felix since he'd come to live with me.

'Thanks again for this,' I said to Vicky as I headed off to meet Rupinder.

As arranged, Rupinder and I met in the car park so we could walk in together.

'How are you feeling now?' Rupinder asked me.

'I'm absolutely fine, but I've felt wiped out since yesterday,' I told her. 'I think it's all the adrenalin wearing off.'

We walked through the hospital corridors together until we found the psychiatric ward. It was a secure unit so we had to buzz in.

A nurse led us to a reception area where we signed in and she then took us to an office. I'd been to a psychiatric ward before and I knew that you didn't have access to the actual ward. When you came to visit patients, you generally saw them in the visitors' room.

There was a desk with two chairs in front of it, so Rupinder and I sat on those and waited for the psychiatrist to arrive. A few minutes later, a tall, dark-haired woman came in.

'I'm Dr Jenny Pickard,' she smiled. 'I'm one of the consultant psychiatrists here.'

Rupinder introduced us both.

'Thank you for taking the time to meet with us,' I said.

'My pleasure,' she replied. 'As there's no immediate family around, I thought it would be helpful to update you both in person.'

'How's Emily doing?' asked Rupinder.

Dr Pickard described how she'd been quite agitated and aggressive when she'd first been brought in and they'd had to restrain and then sedate her for her own safety. She was currently under 24-hour observation.

My heart sank at the thought of Emily having to be restrained and how frightened she must have been feeling.

'She was behaving very oddly the other day,' Rupinder told her. 'It culminated in her taking her baby who, as you know, is currently in Social Services' care. It suddenly became clear to us that she was having a breakdown and was very mentally unstable.'

'You're right in that it is a breakdown, but we believe that she has a specific mental illness that's triggered by childbirth,' nodded Dr Pickard.

'We did wonder whether she was suffering from postnatal depression or the baby blues,' I said.

'I'm afraid this is way beyond the baby blues,' said Dr Pickard.

She explained that Emily had been diagnosed with something called postpartum psychosis.

We listened intently as she explained that it was a severe mental illness that happened suddenly in the days and weeks after having a baby. It caused the rapid onset of psychotic symptoms, including hallucinations and delusions, bizarre behaviour, mania, confusion and depression – so many of the things that Emily had been exhibiting.

'One minute, mums can be manic, full of energy and plans, the next they can be very down and scared, hearing voices or messages and being very paranoid and suicidal,' she explained. 'Sadly, they can become very frightened of their baby. Some sufferers believe their baby has been possessed or that they're out to hurt them in some way.'

It was horrific.

'It's a condition that can get worse really quickly and it needs to be treated as a medical emergency,' she told us. 'Tragically I've seen several cases where a mum has taken their own life and sometimes their baby's life too.'

I shuddered to think how differently this could have all ended if Emily had managed to get Felix to the train station.

'Emily's sister said she didn't have a history of mental illness,' said Rupinder. 'She's never been diagnosed with anxiety or depression or anything like that.'

'You don't have to have had a previous diagnosis,' Dr Pickard told us. 'Research shows you're more at risk if you're bipolar or schizophrenic but, like Emily, that's not necessarily the case.'

She explained that it could affect women days after giving birth or up to six or seven weeks afterwards.

'More research needs to be done on it,' she added. 'But we

see a lot of women like Emily who've had a long, traumatic birth and then go straight into looking after a newborn, so they're not getting any sleep.'

'When I think about what she was experiencing, she must have felt so frightened,' I sighed.

'She's in the right place now,' nodded the doctor. 'Some women with postpartum psychosis can be treated in a mother and baby unit, which often works really well as they can keep their babies with them.'

'Is that not an option for Emily?' asked Rupinder.

'Not at present, I'm afraid,' she told us. 'She's too poorly.'

'So what happens now?' asked Rupinder.

'She needs time,' Dr Pickard told us. 'Time for the medication to start working, for her to heal and get better.'

She explained that Emily had been put on antipsychotics, mood stabilisers and a sedative to help her sleep.

'It's not going to be instant in a severe case like this,' she warned. 'It's going to be a long road. However, most woman diagnosed with postpartum psychosis do go on to make a full recovery.'

It was both devastating and frightening to hear that someone could become so unwell so quickly and severely.

'I'll contact Emily's sister in New Zealand and explain what's happening,' replied Rupinder.

'If she wants to call me, I'd be more than happy to speak to her and explain the situation directly,' offered Dr Pickard.

I was keen to know what the situation might be with Felix.

'Do you think we might be able to bring her baby up to the hospital so Emily can see him?' I asked.

Dr Pickard shook her head.

'She's not able to see visitors right now,' she told us. 'It will take time for the medication to kick in and for Emily to stabilise. She's pretty groggy and out of it at the moment.'

'Perhaps we can reassess the situation in a few days?' added Rupinder.

'Most definitely,' she nodded. 'We've got to take it day by day right now.'

I left the hospital that morning with a heavy heart. I knew from my frightening experience the other day that Emily was very ill, but hearing about the symptoms of postpartum psychosis was terrifying.

'Poor Emily,' I sighed to Rupinder as we walked out to the car park together. 'So what happens now?'

'I don't think we can do anything but press pause on the whole situation for a few weeks,' shrugged Rupinder. 'It sounds like Emily's too ill for anyone to make any decisions about her future, or Felix's.'

For the moment, it was the only option.

When I got back, Vicky could tell I was upset.

'Oh, Maggie,' she asked, concerned. 'What happened at the hospital?'

As she was a fellow foster carer, I knew I could be honest with her and that she would keep things confidential.

'Poor Emily's really ill,' I sighed.

I told Vicky about postpartum psychosis and how the consultant had described it.

'I've heard of postnatal depression but nothing like that,' Vicky said. 'I didn't realise that could happen after giving birth.'

'No, me neither,' I agreed.

In a way, I was reassured that it wasn't just Rupinder and I who'd been ignorant of the condition.

'Poor love,' sighed Vicky. 'She sounds really poorly.'

'I think she's got a long road ahead of her,' I agreed.

It had helped to chat things over with Rupinder and now Vicky, and at least I knew what we were facing.

I also wanted to say something to Amena as she needed to know what was going on and was bound to ask me how long Felix was going to be staying with us. She was also old enough to understand that some people suffered from mental health problems.

'Felix's mum has gone into hospital as she had a breakdown,' I told her when she got home from school.

'Oh,' she said. 'That's sad.'

'Hopefully she'll be OK but it's going to take a bit of time,' I told her.

'Does that mean Felix is going to stay with us?' she asked.

'For now, yes,' I nodded.

My worry was, the more time that Emily spent apart from her son, the less likely she was to bond with him. If that bond had been broken, could it ever be repaired?

ELEVEN

Life Goes On

A few days later, some good news finally emerged from the dark reality of Emily's situation. Rupinder called me one afternoon to say the police had been in touch.

'They've decided they're not going to press any charges against Emily for abandoning Felix,' she told me.

'I should hope not, now we know how ill she was at the time,' I replied. 'She clearly wasn't in her right mind.'

Rupinder had told them about the postpartum psychosis diagnosis and given them Dr Pickard's contact details in case they needed her to confirm this.

She also told me that the hospital social worker had been in touch, and they were going to go to Emily's flat together to get some of her things. Emily had given permission and handed them her keys.

'She said it's always nice for patients to have their own pyjamas and clothes instead of hospital-issue stuff,' she told me.

'That sounds like a good idea,' I said. 'I'm happy to put together a toiletry bag for her or I can nip to the supermarket and get her whatever else she needs?'

It seemed that Emily had no one and I wanted her to know that she had support; that there were people who were there for her.

Rupinder was also going to see if there was anything at the flat that Felix might need.

'We're going tomorrow so I'll bring anything round to you afterwards,' she told me.

I didn't think any more of it until the following afternoon when I pulled up at my house to see Rupinder sitting outside in her car.

I lifted Felix out of the back and walked over to her.

'I'm so sorry,' I said. 'I didn't realise you were coming. We've just been to the supermarket.'

'It's my fault for not letting you know,' she told me. 'I just called round on the off chance.'

She helped me carry my shopping bags inside and I flicked the kettle on to make us a coffee.

I liked Rupinder and I could tell straight away that she wasn't her usual bubbly self.

'Is everything OK?' I asked her.

'Yeah, it's fine,' she shrugged. 'I've just been to Emily's flat with the hospital social worker.'

'How did it go?' I asked.

Rupinder suddenly looked as if she was going to burst into tears.

'Oh, Maggie, it was awful,' she said. 'It gave me an insight into how ill she really was and how her mind had just unravelled.'

'Oh no, was it a mess?' I asked, but she shook her head.

She described what a lovely flat it was and how it was all beautifully decorated.

'There was a gorgeous nursery with navy blue walls and a thick cream rug and a stripy armchair and matching blind,' she told me. 'It looked like something you'd see in a magazine. But she'd obviously got rid of Felix's things as there was nothing in there – no clothes, no cot, no nappies or any baby equipment. In fact, the doorway was all taped up so we had to break through it to get inside.'

She also described how every radiator in the flat was covered in bubble wrap or taped up with bin bags, and the same with the TV.

'To try to stop the voices that she was hearing . . .' I said sadly.

Rupinder also told me how the walls were covered in pages and pages of lists and Post-it notes.

'It was unbelievable,' she sighed. 'I've never seen anything like it.'

'What did they say?' I asked.

'Most of it didn't make sense,' she told me. 'There were lots of escape plans and pages of notes about Felix's feeding times and nappy changes and routines.'

She described how 'leave me alone' and 'go away' were scrawled on the living room walls in pen.

'I actually took some of the notes down and brought them with me in case they were of any use to the doctors in some way,' she said.

She pulled a pile of notes out of her bag and showed them to me. As I read through them, I felt sick.

Bad things are going to happen. They're watching me through the monitor. If I sleep, I will die. Is that baby one of them? If I sleep, will he die?

That baby is a devil with his evil red eyes. Is he sending them messages? He is telling them where I am.

She pointed out some notes that were about the midwife and us.

The midwife is a fake. I know the social worker and foster carer are actors. They are all in on it. They are watching me through the cameras.

I have a higher knowledge and power. The only way to save us is to die.

It was utterly heartbreaking to read. You could feel the desperation in Emily's words and I could see why Rupinder was so upset.

'How did we not realise how ill she was?' she sighed.

It was a question that had been nagging away at me.

'I have no idea,' I replied. 'But at least we know now.'

That afternoon, Rupinder emailed Dr Pickard with all the information. She messaged her back to say Emily was still very out of it and catatonic as her body adjusted to the medication.

'There is one good thing though,' Rupinder told me. 'She said Emily's no longer under 24-hour observation'

'That's progress,' I replied.

I was so worried about her, but we had to cling on to the hope that eventually she would come through it. Until then, life went on and her little boy was growing bigger and stronger.

Felix was ten weeks old now and it seemed like every few days he was doing something new.

One Friday I was looking after Edie, so I met Vicky at a local toddler group in the church hall.

While Paige and Edie were off playing together, I put Felix on his front on a playmat for some tummy time.

'Gosh, he's so strong,' said Vicky. 'Look how he's holding his head and shoulders up.'

'He really is,' I smiled. 'I'm sure he's going to roll soon.'

Felix was really vocal too. He was still cooing and babbling away, and more and more smiles were coming every day.

'Can I have a cuddle?' asked Vicky.

'Of course you can,' I said.

She scooped him up and put him on her lap. She chatted to him and he was cooing away and blowing spit bubbles.

'Try to make him smile again,' I told her. 'I want to get a photo.'

I was determined to get a photo of him smiling so I could put it in the book that I'd started for Emily. Every milestone he reached or new thing that he did, I made sure I documented it.

I hoped that one day Emily would have a chance to read it and catch up on all that she had missed out on. It was also important for Felix to have these memories recorded for when he was older. Children loved to see photos of themselves as babies or toddlers but children in the care system often didn't have them. There were often huge chunks of their early lives missing. Whatever happened to Felix in the future, I wanted this part of his life to be recorded so he could see what he looked like as a newborn and know when he first smiled, sat up or took his first steps.

One of my pet hates was when primary schools asked children to bring in photos of themselves when they were little or got them to do a family tree. Many children in the care system don't know their family tree and neither does their foster carer. I'd been up to my local primary school so many times and told them how traumatising and distressing it was for looked-after children. Thankfully, in response to this, they'd now stopped doing it.

My mind was so taken up with worrying about Emily and Felix that I was surprised one afternoon to get a phone call from Amena's social worker, Rachel.

'I haven't spoken to you for ages,' I told her. 'How are things?'

'Maggie, I'm afraid I've got some bad news,' she told me. 'I've just had a phone call from Amena's mum, Hodan.'

My heart sank.

'I'm afraid that her aunt died this morning.'

'Oh no,' I gasped. 'I'm really sorry.'

Amena knew her aunt had run out of treatment options and was on palliative care, but it would still be a shock for her.

Rachel explained that Hodan was going to call Amena after school and tell her the news.

'I wanted to let you know beforehand to make sure that you were with Amena in case she's upset or needs any extra support.'

'Of course,' I said.

I knew Amena had grown up with her aunt, but while she and Hodan had moved to the UK, Amena's aunt had gone to France and Amena hadn't seen much of her in the past few years.

'How was Hodan when you spoke to her?' I asked.

'Naturally she was very upset but I think there's also a part of her that's relieved as her sister had been ill for so long.'

'Do you know when the funeral might be?' I asked, my mind whirring, thinking about how to get Amena to France.

'It's happening this evening,' Rachel told me.

Although Amena wasn't particularly religious, her family were Muslim and I knew they believed in burying people within twenty-four hours of their death.

'Hodan knows that Amena won't be able to get over in time,' Rachel told me. 'She's going to tie up a few loose ends in France and then head back to the UK.'

My mind had been so focused on her aunt's death that I hadn't thought of the implications. If Hodan was coming back to the UK, this meant Amena would be leaving my house and going to live with her.

While I was happy for Amena, it was a bit of a shock for me. I'd got used to her being here and I loved having her around. I knew Louisa and Edie had grown very fond of her too.

'Do you think Amena will be leaving straight away?' I asked Rachel.

When Hodan had realised that she was going to be in France for a while, the council had made her give up her flat.

'It depends on the housing situation,' said Rachel. 'When Hodan gets back, she'll have to go into temporary or emergency housing at first.'

She went on to explain that Social Services would contact the housing department and request that Amena and Hodan were on the priority list so they could finally live together again.

'Your guess is as good as mine as to how long that could take,' said Rachel.

'OK,' I said. 'We'll have to take it as it comes. You know Amena can stay here for as long as she needs to.'

Rachel arranged to check in with me later to see how Amena was doing.

*

It felt strange waiting for Amena to come home from school, knowing that her mother would be calling with bad news. I knew it was important that the news came from Hodan so I had to carry on and pretend that everything was normal. I hated keeping things from her but I understood it was for the right reasons.

When Amena got back from school, I got her a drink and she was just having a cuddle with Felix when her phone rang.

'Oh, it's my mum,' she said.

I quickly lifted Felix off her knee and went to get his bouncer from the living room to give Amena a bit of space.

When I came back in, she was already off the phone and was sat at the kitchen table, quietly sobbing.

'My aunt died today,' she wept. 'My mum just told me.'

'Oh, lovey, I'm so sorry,' I told her. I went over and gave her a hug.

'How's your mum doing?' I asked, sitting down next to her.

'She's really sad. She was trying to be brave for me but I could tell she was crying.' She described how her mum had been with her aunt at the hospice when she'd passed away.

'She was holding her hand,' she sobbed.

I put my arm around her. 'I bet that brought your aunt so much comfort to know that her sister was there with her,' I soothed.

I made Amena a cup of tea and we sat and chatted.

'There's some good news though,' she said. 'Mum needs to sort out my aunt's flat but then she's coming back – for good this time.'

'That's wonderful,' I smiled, hiding my own sadness.

'Can I go and live with her again?' she asked me.

'Of course you can,' I said. 'We'll have to chat to Rachel about timings and your mum will need to sort out somewhere for you both to live but hopefully that won't take long.'

'I feel bad that I'm happy,' Amena sighed.

'You're bound to be happy,' I said. 'Your mum's coming home after so long – that really is something to celebrate. Your aunt would be happy that you can be together again.'

Amena nodded.

'I'm going to miss living here with you though,' she sighed. 'And Felix.'

'And we're going to miss you too,' I smiled.

'So many kids have left since I've been here and now it's my turn,' she said.

Amena disappeared off upstairs to her bedroom and I dropped Rachel a quick message.

She's OK. She's upset but also excited about her mum coming back and going to live with her again.

I wanted to give Amena a little bit of space and time on her own. Eventually Felix nodded off in his bouncer so twenty minutes later, I went upstairs to check on her.

Much to my surprise, Amena had emptied everything in her drawers and wardrobe out onto her bed and there was stuff strewn all over the room.

'What are you doing, lovey?' I asked her.

'Packing,' she told me. 'Mum said she's going to be back in a few days so I need to be ready.'

'Do you think I could have a goodbye tea with Louisa and Edie before I go?' she continued as she tipped out the contents of her bedside table. 'We could get pizza or you could make my favourite pasta?'

I could see how excited Amena was and I didn't want to disappoint her, but she needed to know the truth.

Moving a pile of jumpers to one side, I sat down on her bed.

'I know your mum's coming back, flower, but in reality, it might be a while before you're able to go and live with her again,' I told her.

'But Rachel will help us get a new flat,' Amena replied.

'Even if Social Services do write to the housing department and ask for you to be a priority, the waiting lists can be very long,' I warned her. 'Sometimes it can be months before a suitable property comes up.'

I didn't like to say it to Amena but I knew families who had waited for over a year to be offered a suitable property.

'Months?' gasped Amena. 'But that's not fair.'

'I know,' I sighed. 'But it's the way things are unfortunately. I just want you to be aware that your mum might be in temporary accommodation for a while.'

Amena looked downcast.

'Can I go and live with her at a hostel then?' she asked.

'Your mum will probably just be given a single room if she gets a place at a hostel,' I explained. 'And often these places aren't ideal for children.'

In some hostels, children weren't even allowed.

'I think the plan is for you to stay here until the council can get you both a suitable place to live. So don't worry, you've got plenty of time to sort your stuff out.'

Amena looked like she was going to cry and I felt guilty for destroying her hopes, but it was important for her to know the reality of the situation. She was going to be with me and Felix for a little while yet.

TWELVE

Patience

A few days later, Hodan was back in the UK. The local authority had found her a temporary place in a hostel on the other side of town.

Amena was desperate to see her.

'Can I go and meet her after school?' she asked.

'I don't see why not as long as you run it by Rachel,' I said.

Amena had only come into the care system voluntarily because her mum had had to leave the country. Hodan's parenting had never been under question, so Amena was entitled to see her as often as she wanted.

However, when she came home that evening, I could see she was upset.

'The hostel was horrible,' she told me. 'It's run-down and noisy and there were people drinking and smoking.'

'Your poor mum,' I said.

'She was really frightened, so she just stays in her room,' she said.

It wasn't ideal, but Social Services had written to the

housing department to explain Hodan's situation and ask if they could be made a priority.

I knew Amena wanted to spend as much time as possible with her mum, but it sounded like the hostel wasn't an ideal place for her to visit.

'Do you think your mum would like to come over for dinner tomorrow night?' I asked her.

'Really?' grinned Amena. 'I think she would love that. I'll get some halal chicken and I can make food for us all,' she said excitedly.

'That sounds lovely,' I smiled.

When Hodan arrived the following evening, she threw her arms around me. She was a tiny woman and so warm and loving.

'I'm so sorry about your sister,' I told her.

'Thank you,' she replied. 'She went peacefully in the end. Though I should be the one thanking you for taking such good care of my little girl,' she said, squeezing my hand.

'I've loved having her,' I smiled. 'And I'm so pleased you two can be together again.'

Hodan ended up rolling her sleeves up and helping Amena make dinner. It was lovely to watch them cooking together and I could see how pleased Amena was to have her mum back.

After we'd tucked into a tasty Somali stew with chicken and chickpeas, Hodan and Amena watched a film while I put Felix to bed.

I came downstairs to find them snuggled up on the sofa together.

'The baby is sleeping?' asked Hodan.

'Yes,' I smiled. 'He's such a good boy. He always goes down without any trouble.'

'He's cute isn't he, Momma?' smiled Amena.

'Just like you were, my little princess,' Hodan told her, giving her a hug.

I could tell how hard it was for both of them when Hodan had to leave to get the bus back to the hostel.

I felt guilty for not offering for her to stay the night, but I had Felix here and she hadn't been police-checked. Also, as a foster carer, I felt it was important for me to keep professional boundaries. Hodan wasn't a friend or a family member; she was what Social Services called a client. As much as I would have liked to offer her a bed for the night to get away from the hostel, it wasn't really appropriate to ask her to stay over. I was happy for her to come round here and spend time with Amena though.

'I was thinking about making a roast on Sunday,' I told Hodan. 'Would you like to come round? Perhaps you could spend the afternoon here?'

Amena looked at her mum and smiled.

'Thank you, I would enjoy that,' nodded Hodan.

Seeing these two together that night, I put aside any sadness that I'd felt about Amena leaving. They had such a strong bond and it was heartening to see how happy Amena was to have her mother back in her life again.

Rupinder contacted me a few days later with an update.

'The hospital's been in touch,' she said. 'They've suggested that we bring Felix in to see Emily.'

'That's great news,' I smiled. 'If she wants to see him, that must mean she's making progress.'

'I don't think we should expect too much,' Rupinder replied. 'But let's see how it goes.'

Despite Rupinder's words, I felt really positive about taking Felix up to the hospital. Hopefully now the medication had kicked in, Emily was starting to feel more like her old self.

'You might get a cuddle with Mummy today,' I told Felix as I changed his nappy and put him in a new outfit.

He gave me a gummy smile back and it struck me that Emily was going to notice how much he'd changed since she'd last seen him just a few weeks ago.

He was getting so big; he'd grown out of all his newborn babygros and was already in three-to-six-month clothes.

Like the last time, I met Rupinder in the hospital car park.

'Doesn't he look cute!' she smiled as she saw Felix in his little blue leggings and stripy top.

'I wanted him to look nice for his mummy,' I told her.

We made our way down the maze of hospital corridors to the psychiatric ward.

'Do you think we'll be in the visitors' room this time?' I asked Rupinder.

'Because this is more like a contact session and there's a baby involved, I did ask if they could find us our own room,' she told me.

Sure enough, we were directed to an empty office like the one we'd spoken to Dr Pickard in.

'If you wait here, someone will bring Emily through,' a nurse told us.

I got Felix out of his car seat and sat him on my knee.

'I should have brought his playmat or some toys or something,' I sighed. 'I didn't think.'

I'd brought my changing bag with me, with nappies, wipes and a bottle in case he needed a feed, but nothing else.

'He'll be OK,' said Rupinder. 'Hopefully Emily might want to hold him.'

'Oh, that would be amazing,' I smiled.

We waited and waited. The clock ticked but there was still no sign of Emily or a nurse. Felix started to get restless so I paced up and down and showed him some of the posters on the wall and pointed to the leaves on the trees outside that were blowing in the wind.

'Do you think she's coming?' I asked Rupinder.

We'd been waiting for nearly twenty minutes by then.

'I'll just nip out to reception and check,' she said.

I bounced Felix on my lap and sang him a nursery rhyme.

'Mummy will be here soon,' I smiled, really hoping that it was true.

A few seconds later, Rupinder was back.

'She's coming now apparently,' she told me, and I felt a huge sense of relief as well as anticipation.

A few minutes later, the door pushed open and a nurse came in followed by Emily. I was taken aback by how different she looked.

Even when she was at her most unwell, I'd only ever seen Emily fully made-up and smartly dressed. But she was shuffling along towards us in a grey dressing gown and slippers, her hair greasy and scraped back into a ponytail, her face very pale with dark shadows under her eyes. She looked like she hadn't slept in a long while.

'I'm Allie, one of the mental health nurses here at the unit,' the nurse told us.

Rupinder introduced us both.

'And this is Emily's son, Felix,' I smiled.

'What a handsome boy you've got, Emily,' Allie told her.

Emily nodded but stared down at the ground. There was an empty chair next to me and Felix, but she shuffled over to a chair next to Rupinder instead.

The last time I'd seen Emily, she'd looked so poorly. I'd never forget the vacant, glassy blackness in her eyes. I'd been hoping to come today and see a huge improvement. But now she just seemed broken – like the shell of a person.

'How are you feeling, Emily?' Rupinder asked her.

'OK, thank you,' she nodded, still not making eye contact with anybody.

I could see that she was physically shaking.

My heart sank. I'd been hoping that she would want to hold Felix but I could see that I'd been naïve. Her recovery was going to take time.

'I hope you don't mind but I brought you a few little things,' I told her.

I passed a bag with some magazines, a crossword puzzle book and a small box of chocolates over to Rupinder. Rupinder put it down on the floor next to Emily's chair.

'Thank you,' she said, looking down at her feet.

There was an awkward silence in the room as everyone struggled to know what to say.

'Your son is so strong,' I told Emily. 'He's holding his head up now and I think he's going to roll over any day soon.'

'He loves his playmat, doesn't he, Maggie?' added Rupinder.

'That's right,' I nodded. 'He likes the black and white shapes, and I bet it won't be long before he starts trying to grab them.'

Emily was gazing off into the distance, jiggling her leg up and down. I wasn't sure if she was even listening to what we were saying. Suddenly Felix started to cry and wriggle on my lap.

'Shhh shhh,' I soothed as I bounced him up and down. I faced him out instead of inwards so he could see the rest of the room.

'Look, there's Mummy,' I told him. 'Mummy's come to see you.'

Felix let out a loud wail and Emily looked terrified. She crossed her arms across her chest and hunched over in her chair, shaking.

'Are you OK, Emily?' Allie asked her. 'Do you want me to get you a glass of water?'

Felix was really crying now and I was doing my best to soothe him.

Emily suddenly leapt to her feet.

'I'm sorry, I can't do this,' she mumbled as she ran out of the room.

Allie quickly went after her.

All the positivity I'd felt about this visit had vanished in seconds. I didn't know what I'd been expecting but I'd at least hoped Emily would have taken an interest in Felix or wanted to ask questions about him.

'I didn't even have a chance to give her the photos,' I sighed.

I'd brought an envelope containing a handful of photos that I'd taken of Felix over the past few weeks and I'd written the milestones on the back of them – one was his first smile, one of him on his playmat and when he first turned his head to a sound.

'She doesn't seem that much better,' I sighed. 'She still seemed very out of it and zombie-like.'

'Her body will still be adjusting to all of the medication,' nodded Rupinder.

I felt so heartbroken for Emily as she was still clearly very unwell.

'What do we do now?' I asked her. 'Do we just go?'

'I think so,' shrugged Rupinder. 'I can't see Emily coming back and Allie's probably with her.'

I felt so disheartened as I strapped Felix back into his car seat.

As we walked down the corridor, we heard Allie coming after us. We sat down in the reception area with her.

'I think that was very hard for Emily,' she said. 'We had talked it through beforehand and she'd said she wanted to see Felix, but she really struggled.'

'What's she struggling with in particular?' asked Rupinder.

'I think she's frightened of him,' said Allie. 'I know she was finding it really difficult to be in the same room as him.'

She explained that although she didn't have the psychosis anymore, there was still part of her that saw Felix as something to be feared.

'I think he triggers her into remembering how she was feeling for the past few weeks and I think she's also very scared of him somehow hurting her or her hurting him.'

It was so sad to hear.

'How do you think she can get through this?' asked Rupinder.

'Time, medication, therapy,' shrugged Allie. 'As Dr Pickard's probably already warned you, Emily's got a long road ahead of her. We just have to be patient.'

I left the hospital that day feeling thoroughly deflated. If Emily couldn't even bear to be in the same room as her son for more than a few minutes, was she ever going to get to a place where she felt comfortable caring for him full-time?

I could see Rupinder was thinking the same.

'What do we do now?' I asked her as we stood by my car in the car park.

'We try again another time,' she shrugged. 'And we keep trying until Emily starts to come through this.'

But would she ever come through this?

I looked down at Felix in his car seat. For his sake, I really hoped that she could. However, at this point in time, I just didn't know.

THIRTEEN

Baby Steps

After the disastrous first visit, Dr Pickard asked Rupinder and I to come back to the hospital to see her.

'I heard what happened the other day,' she told us. 'And I think we need to give it a bit more time before we bring Felix in to see Emily again. In hindsight, I think it was too soon.'

She explained that they were trying to get Emily to focus on completing small, manageable tasks each day.

'That could be something as simple as having a shower or getting dressed,' she explained. 'Or taking part in an arts and crafts session or going for a five-minute walk outside with one of the nurses.'

Slow and steady was the aim, especially when it came to Felix.

'Let's wait a week or so and see how she is,' Dr Pickard told us. 'We're hoping that she'll start to open up a lot more through talking therapy and some of the group activities, but it's important to remember it's still very early days.'

She explained that the antipsychotics had helped to control Emily's symptoms but that they didn't instantly cure the underlying condition.

'The hallucinations, delusional thoughts and confusion have gone, but it could be several days or weeks and some different medication before we see the full effect,' she told us. 'So Emily still has a long way to go.'

'Is she starting to take more of an interest in Felix?' Rupinder asked.

'At present, she doesn't talk much about the baby or ask about him,' said Dr Pickard. 'But as time goes by, and things start to settle, I'm hoping that will start to change. Sadly, she's very frightened of him and I think it's triggering for her to see him because it takes her right back to how she felt before.'

'She was absolutely terrified,' I sighed, remembering the awful day she'd been sectioned.

Dr Pickard also wanted to reduce the length of the visits but make them more frequent.

'If we said it was only going to be for ten minutes then I think that would help Emily feel able to cope,' she told us. 'She would know it's just a short, manageable period of time that she has to spend in the same room as the baby.'

Then hopefully we could build it up from there.

'However, I also appreciate that it might not be convenient for you coming all the way over here for ten minutes, two or three times a week,' Dr Pickard added.

'I'm happy to do whatever it takes to help Emily try to bond with Felix,' I nodded. 'And I'm assuming we wouldn't necessarily need Rupinder to come every time?'

I was aware that she probably wouldn't be able to commit to multiple visits a week alongside meetings and all the other cases that she was juggling.

'I'm happy for you to come on your own, Maggie, if that works for you?' replied Rupinder.

'One of the nurses will always be present too,' Dr Pickard told us.

I was someone who liked a plan and it seemed that we had one, and were at least moving in the right direction.

With the 'pause' button pressed yet again, life carried on. Felix kept me busy and Hodan was spending several evenings a week at my house with Amena. I didn't mind at all. There was still no update about any suitable housing, and I knew how much she disliked the hostel and how happy it made Amena having her mum back in her life.

Ten days after our first visit to the hospital to see Emily, Rupinder called.

'They want to try again,' she told me. 'Would you be able to take Felix to see Emily tomorrow?'

'Of course,' I replied.

This time, as I drove up to the hospital, I had very low expectations.

'Let's see how it goes shall we, Felix?' I said, lifting him out of the car.

Would Emily be able to stay in the same room as him for ten minutes? After the last time, I wasn't so sure.

I'd come more prepared for this visit and I put Felix on the floor on a change mat with a few toys around him. I hoped this meant there was less chance of him getting bored and unsettled.

Thankfully, I didn't have to wait too long for Emily and Allie to appear. When Emily walked in, I was surprised to see that she'd got dressed. She was wearing a jumper and tracksuit bottoms, and her long hair was wet and I could see it had been freshly washed. She still looked pale and utterly exhausted.

As she came in, she momentarily looked up and made eye contact with me.

'Hi, Emily,' I smiled. 'It's good to see you.'

I didn't want her to feel any pressure to interact with me or Felix, so Allie and I chatted. Emily seemed more focused on picking at her fingernails but, at one point, I noticed her glancing at Felix as he babbled away on the floor.

'He's very noisy, isn't he?' laughed Allie.

'He really is,' I smiled. 'He's always chatting away.'

Emily was shifting around in her seat and I could tell that she was starting to get panicky. Allie must also have picked up on her unease.

'I think it's been ten minutes,' she said loudly. 'Shall we take you back to your room, Emily?'

'Yes, please,' she nodded, jumping up.

Emily didn't say anything as she followed Allie out of the room, but as she walked out of the door, I saw her give Felix a little backwards glance. However, when she caught me watching her, she quickly looked away.

I promised Rupinder that I'd call her with an update when I got home.

'How did it go?' she asked.

'Well, Emily stayed in the same room as Felix for ten minutes,' I said. 'But that was about it.'

'I think that's all we can hope for at this stage,' she replied.

It was frustrating but I had to remember that old-fashioned saying: slow and steady wins the race.

Over the years, I'd dealt with a lot of birth parents who had mental health issues so I knew the road to getting back to some sort of normality was never straightforward and that there were many ups and downs along the way.

One morning, three days later, I was about to put Felix in the car to take him up to the hospital when my phone rang. It was Allie.

'Emily's not too good,' she told me. 'I'm sorry, but I think we'd better leave it for today.'

She explained that she'd been really struggling and hadn't got out of bed.

'That's OK,' I said brightly. 'We have to take each day as it comes.'

We couldn't force Emily to see her son and she had to be in a good headspace herself before she could even try to be a mother to Felix.

'Let's see how she goes and perhaps try again in a few days,' said Allie.

Rupinder was receiving regular updates from the hospital and this week it definitely sounded as if Emily was experiencing a dip in mood.

'Apparently it's to be expected,' Rupinder told me. 'They're going to try tweaking her medication.'

By the following week, things were back on track so I took Felix to the hospital for a visit.

My heart sank when Emily came into the room wearing her dressing gown, and her hair looked as if it hadn't seen a brush for a while. But there was colour in her cheeks and her eyes looked more expressive somehow.

I was holding Felix on my knee and I was taken aback when Emily came and sat next to me. Normally she picked the chair that was furthest away from her son.

Like before, she didn't say much and I didn't want to force her to make conversation so Allie and I chatted. Felix had fallen asleep in my arms and we were talking about a drama we'd both watched on TV when suddenly, out of the corner of my eye, I noticed Emily's hand reach out towards him. I held my breath as she tenderly stroked his head.

'He's got such thick hair,' she sighed. 'It was like that when he was born. The midwife commented on what a lovely colour it was.'

'It's the same colour as yours,' I smiled.

'Do you think so?' she asked, surprised.

'Definitely,' I nodded. 'It's a gorgeous chestnut brown.'

Touching his hair was just a tiny gesture but it felt like huge progress. Buoyed by that success, I turned to Emily.

'Would you like to hold him?' I asked her. 'I'm sure Felix would love to have a cuddle with his mummy.' As soon as the words had left my mouth, I regretted saying them.

Emily quickly pulled her hand away.

'No,' she mumbled. 'No, thank you.'

Allie gave me a sympathetic smile as if to say *don't worry* but I was annoyed at myself for pushing her. I knew we had to let Emily take the lead and do things in her own time and I hoped that I hadn't scared her off.

'I think it's time to head back now, Emily,' Allie told her gently.

I glanced at the clock and realised that we'd been there for nearly twenty minutes. I got up to put Felix back into his car seat.

'Thank you for bringing him,' said Emily quietly. 'Maybe I could hold him another time?'

'Of course you can,' I told her. 'He's your son, you can hold him whenever you want to.'

'Thank you,' she said, giving me a weak smile.

I left the hospital that day feeling a spark of hope. Perhaps things were finally improving?

When I got home, I called Rupinder and told her what had happened.

'I can't believe I pushed her like that,' I sighed. 'I should have known better.'

'Maggie, don't beat yourself up about it,' she replied. 'It was coming from a good place.'

She was keen to check in with Emily, so she was going to accompany me on the next visit.

This time, when we arrived at the hospital, I was surprised to see Allie waiting for us in reception.

'Is everything OK?' I asked her.

'Yes, it's fine,' she said. 'I just wanted to grab you both before today's session.'

She explained that, as part of Dr Pickard's therapy with Emily, they'd been talking about Felix.

'Emily gets very fearful around him,' Allie told us. 'We think he reminds her of everything she's been through.'

She also explained that when she was in the midst of her psychosis, she'd told them how she believed Felix was 'one of them' and was going to hurt her.

Hearing those words made me question whether Emily would ever get over that or if Felix would always remind her of the darkest time in her life. Could she move past that or, if we were being realistic, was adoption going to be the best way forward for him now?

'If you don't feel like her seeing Felix is going to help her at this point in time then we understand,' nodded Rupinder. 'We know that it's going to be a long process.'

'No, not at all,' replied Allie. 'Emily wants to see him and she's specifically said that she would like to try to hold him.'

Rupinder and I looked at each other.

'Are you sure that's a good idea?' Rupinder asked.

'I think it's worth a try and we're all around her for support if it proves to be too much,' added Allie.

She said Emily had talked about it with her and Dr Pickard and it was one of her aims.

'She's keen to give it a go,' she said.

I should have been happy that Emily was finally showing an interest in her son but I felt an underlying sense of anxiety. I don't think I'd fully got over the stress and shock of the day that she'd taken Felix, having to drive her around, desperately worrying about how to get the baby away from her while the agonising wait for an ambulance seemed to go on forever.

As we took Felix into the visitors' room, I knew I had to put my own worries to one side.

Thankfully Felix had slept in the car so he was wide awake and alert. After taking him out of his car seat, I kept him on my knee.

When Allie and Emily came in, Emily sat herself down beside me.

'How are you doing?' I asked her.

'OK, thanks,' she nodded.

'Emily and I have been talking and she would really like to have a hold of Felix,' said Allie. 'Wouldn't you, Emily?'

'Yes,' she nodded. 'I think I'd like to try it.'

'Of course,' added Rupinder.

I suddenly felt very awkward and was keen not to put my foot in it again.

'Do you want to hold him right now or wait a little bit?' I asked her.

'Now's fine,' she shrugged.

I stood up with Felix.

'Be careful, he's a bit of a wriggler these days,' I smiled.

Carefully, I handed Emily her son. As I lowered him into her arms, I could feel her whole body shaking.

'Have you got him?' I asked her.

'I think so,' she said nervously. 'He's got so heavy.'

The three of us tried not to stare as Emily sat there with Felix in her arms. At first, she held him very awkwardly and he started to flex and wriggle.

'Hey, it's OK, little one,' she soothed, adjusting him.

But after a few seconds, I could see her becoming more confident.

She traced his delicate eyebrows and stroked his chubby hands. His fist curled tightly around her finger.

'He's got such perfect little fingernails,' she sighed.

I could see she wasn't shaking anymore and, as the warmth of her son's body relaxed into hers, tears started rolling down her cheeks.

FOURTEEN

New Starts

Seeing Emily holding Felix after so long brought a lump to my throat.

I caught Rupinder's eye and she gave me a smile.

However, it was clear that after a couple of minutes, Emily was starting to panic.

'Please could you take him back?' she asked me.

I could hear the desperation in her voice, so I gently lifted Felix out of her arms.

'How was that?' asked Allie.

'Terrifying,' she sighed. 'But I did it.'

'You should be very proud of yourself,' nodded Rupinder.

From then on, very slowly and gradually, Emily started to show more of an interest in Felix. During one visit, she asked if she could help give him a bottle.

'Of course you can,' I told her.

She still looked very stiff and scared when she was holding Felix, and it was clear that it didn't feel natural to her yet. However, the main thing was that she was prepared to try to give him a bottle, even if it meant holding him for a few minutes.

'I don't remember how to do any of this stuff,' she sighed, as I shook the bottle of formula I'd brought along in the changing bag. 'The first few weeks of Felix's life are all a blur.'

'You'll soon pick it up,' I reassured her.

I showed her how to tilt the bottle so the milk filled the teat and it meant that Felix was less likely to ingest any air. Then I showed her how to wind him on her lap afterwards.

The next time I brought him to the hospital, she offered to change his nappy.

'Be my guest,' I smiled. 'I'm definitely happy to get out of that one.'

The visits grew slightly longer too, although we were still playing it by ear. Emily was still very up and down and had her good days and bad days.

Sometimes I could tell she wasn't in a great place so we'd only stay ten minutes. Other times, we were there up to half an hour or more.

Little by little, Emily was getting used to being around Felix again and I hoped her fear and anxiety around him was easing.

However, in the background, I was aware that the clock was ticking. Emily had been in the hospital for six weeks now and Felix was coming up to sixteen weeks old. He'd recently learnt how to roll and was starting to grab things with his chubby fists – his favourite being a chunk of my hair or my earrings.

Rupinder popped in for a coffee one morning and it was clear that she was under pressure from her manager to start working out what the long-term goal was.

'I think we need to start trying to get a sense from Emily about what she's thinking in terms of Felix and their future,' she told me.

Everything had been put on hold when Emily was sectioned and taken into hospital. But if the plan was still to go for adoption, then the adoption team would need to start putting feelers out for suitable parents. Social Services would try to do it as quickly as possible so they could get Felix settled while he was still a baby.

Rupinder said she was going to start talking to Dr Pickard about broaching it with Emily. However, we were all very conscious of pushing Emily too soon as her mental health was still so up and down.

'I'll keep the conversation going and keep you posted,' she told me.

Becky, my supervising social worker, gave me a ring a few days later.

She'd just had a call with Rupinder and her manager.

'As you probably know, they're starting to explore the next steps for Emily,' she told me.

It was still relatively early days for Emily, but she explained that the hospital had said they would potentially consider discharging her in another four or five weeks.

'Obviously that's a rough guide and it might change,' she said. 'But if Emily carries on as she is now, that's the plan.'

She explained that no one knew Emily's wishes yet in regards to Felix, but Rupinder wanted to be able to talk through the options with her. In time, the hospital would discuss it with Emily too.

'Rupinder seems hopeful that Emily is moving away from the idea of adoption at this stage,' Becky told me. 'What do you think?'

In all honesty, I wasn't sure.

'I'd like to think that's the case,' I replied. 'She's definitely trying to interact with Felix more but she's still very nervous and fearful around him.'

If adoption was no longer Emily's intention and she wanted to look at keeping Felix, it was definitely going to take time for her to renew that bond with him. She would also need some sort of parenting assessment to check that she could care for him and prove that she would be able to cope.

'Social Services feel the best way to assess her would be by asking her to do a mother and baby placement,' Becky told me.

I suddenly realised where the conversation was going.

'Obviously you've been caring for Felix since the beginning and you've also been there for Emily too over these past few weeks,' she added.

She paused.

'So Rupinder was wondering how you'd feel about you doing the placement at your house?'

It would involve Emily moving in with me and Felix when she was discharged from hospital.

'It would be a case of teaching her the basics as well as making sure that her mental health is stable enough so that she can look after Felix and herself independently.'

Becky went on to explain that Emily would be discharged to the community mental health team so she'd have a mental health nurse who would come out to see her and give her ongoing support.

Space certainly wasn't the issue. I knew Amena was going to leave at some point and the other bedroom that I used for fostering, the room that Shola and Jordan had stayed in, was still available.

'If Emily wants to keep Felix, then I'd be more than happy to have the placement at home and support them both as best as I can,' I told her.

I hadn't needed to think about it. Emily had been through so much and there was nothing I would love more than to see her reunited with her baby. However, I knew that if that was what she decided she wanted, she was going to have a hard job on her hands convincing Social Services that she could cope.

'Thank you, Maggie,' replied Becky. 'I think Rupinder was hoping you'd say that so I'll let her know.'

But for now, everything was still up in the air. The first thing that needed to happen was for Rupinder to suss out what Emily was thinking. As it happened, Emily brought it up herself.

One morning, after we'd taken Felix up to the hospital for a visit, she turned to us before we left.

'When can I take Felix home?' she asked Rupinder. 'I keep asking Dr Pickard when they're going to let me go but nobody's got any answers.'

'Is that what you want, Emily?' asked Rupinder. 'Do you want to have Felix back full-time? Because before you went into hospital, you were sure that you wanted him to be adopted.'

Tears filled Emily's eyes and she looked horrified.

'But I was ill and I wasn't thinking straight,' she pleaded. 'I've been thinking about it a lot over the past few weeks and I want my baby back.'

Rupinder nodded.

'You have to be sure,' she told her. 'We don't want you to feel like you're being rushed into making a decision.'

'I am sure,' nodded Emily. 'I want my son back. I just want to get out of here and take him back to our flat, put all of this behind us and get on with our lives.'

'I'm afraid it's not as simple or as straightforward as that,' Rupinder told her. 'When you were very ill, you abandoned Felix at the train station and, as a result of that, you agreed for Felix to come into the care system. On a couple of occasions, you also threatened to harm both him and yourself.'

They were harsh words but Emily needed to hear the truth.

'I know I did those awful things and I'll never forgive myself for that – but I was psychotic,' she wept. 'It wasn't really me. My brain had shut down, but I promise you I'm OK now.'

'Social Services have to be sure of that,' Rupinder explained. 'We have to be certain that Felix will be safe in your care and that you can look after him independently.'

I could see Emily was getting upset.

'I can't believe I have to prove that I can look after my own baby,' she sighed. 'Haven't I been through enough?'

'It's as much about protecting you as well as Felix,' Rupinder told her.

Emily looked devastated.

'So what do I have to do then?' she asked. 'What hoops do I have to jump through if I want to keep him?'

Rupinder explained that after she was discharged, she would have to do a mother and baby placement.

'It's a six-week live-in assessment at a carer's house or at a residential unit where you would go right back to basics about how you'd care for a baby.'

She also explained that in addition, Emily would have to attend sessions with a social worker at a family centre twice a week where she'd talk about her fears and anxieties and what she felt she needed to work on.

Emily looked shocked.

'Can't we just go back to my flat and do it?' she asked.

Rupinder shook her head.

'At first, because of everything you've been through, you'll have to be supervised with Felix 24/7.'

She explained that in a residential unit, she'd be with other mums and babies. Emily and Felix would have their own room or separate flat but they'd be monitored by video, and members of staff would be there to supervise her if she was feeding the baby or changing his nappy.

I could see Emily mulling it over.

'I don't like the idea of a residential unit,' she sighed. 'It feels intrusive and with all those people watching me, it would feel like being in the hospital again.'

'So you'd prefer that you and Felix went to live in a foster-care setting?' asked Rupinder.

'If that's what I have to do, then yes,' nodded Emily.

I glanced over at Rupinder. She obviously knew what I was thinking and gave me a little nod.

'Emily, if you wanted to then I'd be more than happy for you and Felix to do the mother and baby placement at my house,' I told her.

Emily stared at me blankly.

'I honestly won't be offended if that's not what you want,' I added. 'But Felix is already settled at my house, and I would love for you to come and join him.'

She still didn't say anything. For continuity for Felix, I felt this would be the best option but I appreciated that Emily might want a fresh start with a new carer. I had seen her at her lowest point and I knew that she was deeply ashamed of how she had behaved.

'You don't have to make any decisions today,' Rupinder told her. 'Take your time to think it over and, as Maggie said, we would all understand if you'd prefer a fresh start with a new carer.'

Emily shook her head.

'No,' she said suddenly. 'It *is* what I want. I'd like to come to your house to be with Felix. I feel safe with you.'

I smiled. 'That's such a compliment,' I told her. 'I'd be happy to help.'

'Right well that sounds like a decision,' nodded Rupinder. 'We'll start to put a plan in place.'

As Rupinder and I walked out to the car park together, we chatted about the conversation that we'd just had with Emily.

'I'm so pleased that she wants to keep the baby,' I smiled.

Adoption had seemed to be the only solution for Felix at one stage so it was testament to Emily and how far she had come.

'I didn't want to bombard her with too much information but she needs to know the reality of it,' Rupinder told me. 'She's still got a long way to go.'

I think it had been a shock to her that Social Services weren't just going to hand Felix back to her.

'I'll give her time to process everything and then I'll have more of a discussion with Emily about how it's going to work at your house,' Rupinder added.

Ten weeks after Emily had been sectioned, we were invited to the hospital for a discharge meeting. I generally didn't look forward to meetings at hospitals as I'd been to a few that had involved up to twenty people and had gone on for hours.

It definitely wasn't the right environment for a five-month-old baby, so Vicky had kindly agreed to come to my house again to look after Felix.

Thankfully this meeting seemed a manageable size. Rupinder and her manager, Chloe, were there; the hospital social worker; Dr Pickard; Allie – Emily's nurse; Becky and Emily. As she looked around the meeting room, Emily looked absolutely terrified and overwhelmed.

Dr Pickard opened up the discussion.

'I'm pleased to say that we're at a point where we're ready to discharge Emily into the care of the community mental health team,' she said.

She talked about how far Emily had come.

'I'm sure you'd agree, Emily, that you've made good progress but the path to recovery isn't linear, as we know,' Dr Pickard told her. 'And you will probably have a few ups and downs to come.'

She described how they'd hopefully found the right balance of medication and how Emily felt her delusions and psychosis had gone.

'You'll still need to be very closely monitored and you'll have regular check-ins with the community mental health team,' she added.

As it wasn't a Social Services meeting, there wouldn't be long discussions about our next steps.

'From a Social Services perspective, what's been decided?' asked Dr Pickard.

'Emily would like to be assessed to see whether she can have Felix full-time,' Rupinder told her.

Emily nodded.

'I want my baby back,' she said, her voice cracking with emotion. 'I don't want him to be adopted. I want Felix to come and live with me but I know I need to prove to everyone that I can do it and that I'm safe to be around him.'

She needed to prove that to herself too.

Rupinder looked up from her notes.

'We've been talking about the different options over the past few weeks and we've decided that Emily's going to be discharged to Maggie's care under a mother and baby placement.'

Dr Pickard nodded.

'Well, we wish you every luck, Emily,' she told her. 'Postpartum psychosis is a rare and frightening condition. But, as I've always assured you, given the right treatment, you can make a full recovery.'

As I looked over at Emily, I so desperately hoped that was going to be the case.

FIFTEEN

Letting Go

We were expecting a very important visitor. As soon as the knock on the door came, I jumped up to answer it.

'Hi,' I smiled as I opened it to find Emily and her nurse, Allie, stood on my doorstep.

Emily looked terrified and I wasn't surprised. I knew coming to my house was a big deal for her and I could guess what was running through her head. The last time she'd stood on the same doorstep, she was in the midst of a terrifying psychosis and was being restrained by paramedics. I knew it was going to be difficult for her, but it was very important for her to come back here to try to move on.

'How are you doing?' I asked her. 'I know this must be really hard for you.'

'I'm OK,' she nodded. 'I'm feeling a bit wobbly but Allie and I have talked it through.'

'She's doing really well,' said Allie.

I ushered them inside.

'Felix is in the kitchen,' I told them. 'I picked up a new seat for him from the charity shop, which he absolutely loves.'

We walked through to the kitchen and I showed them the inflatable ring that Felix was sitting in; it had lots of textures and crinkly things on it for him to grab and feel.

'He's like a little king on his throne,' smiled Allie.

I could see Emily looking around nervously and I suddenly noticed the baby monitor on the worktop. As it had been something she had been very paranoid about when she was last here, I felt like I ought to say something about it.

'I've still got the baby monitor,' I told her. 'Do you feel OK with it?'

I explained that I only used it at night when Felix was in bed or when he fell asleep in the day and I needed to do something else in another room.

Emily looked embarrassed.

'I'm fine,' she nodded. 'It doesn't bother me now.'

This was the first day of her settling-in period ahead of her moving in at the end of the week. She was only staying for an hour and Allie had come along to support her. The idea was that as each day went by, she'd stay a bit longer and then on the final day, she'd finally be discharged from hospital and move in.

As a first step, I gave Emily a tour of my house so she knew where everything was.

I'd tried to make her bedroom a bit more 'adult' despite the bunk beds. I'd taken the toys out and replaced them with some books, and I'd moved a chair in from my bedroom and put a plain white duvet set on the single bed. I'd also put a small TV on top of the chest of drawers in case Emily wanted to have a bit of space away from Amena and I in the evenings.

'It's lovely,' she said. 'But where is the cot?'

I explained that to start off with, Felix would still be sleeping in with me and we'd build things up slowly from there.

'If he wakes up in the night then I'll come and get you and we can try and settle him together, or we'll go downstairs and you can give him a bottle,' I told her. 'But to be honest, now he's older, that's happening less anyway.'

I expected Emily to be upset or seem disheartened but the look on her face was almost one of relief.

'OK,' she said matter-of-factly.

'It's not about trusting you, you know. It's about making sure you can cope and giving you that support at first,' I told her.

I knew it was going to be a big change from the regimented routine and safety of the hospital where Emily had had support around her 24/7.

We went back downstairs and had a cup of tea with Allie, who was holding Felix.

'Do you want a cuddle?' she asked Emily.

'I'm OK at the moment but I will later when I've drunk my tea,' she told her.

Emily still seemed nervous and unsure around Felix, and I knew it was something that I needed to keep an eye on.

After an hour, I could see that Emily was exhausted. We'd all agreed that it was important to take things slowly at first so it wasn't too overwhelming.

Allie drove her over to my house the following day and they stayed a little bit longer this time. On the third day, Emily was due to catch the bus to my house on her own. Allie had mapped out the route and talked her through it, but I could tell that she was dreading it.

'You can do this,' Allie told her.

'And you've got both of our phone numbers if you're really struggling,' I added.

The next morning, Emily was late and she looked shaken up when she arrived – but the main thing was she'd managed to get to my house by herself.

'Everything feels so strange after being in hospital for so long,' Emily told me. 'It's so intense – the noises and the smells and all the people everywhere.'

'It's bound to be a big adjustment at first, but the main thing is you did it,' I smiled.

The furthest Emily had been in the outside world in months was a walk to the shops or around the hospital grounds, usually accompanied by a nurse. However, she was doing so well this week. I was particularly reassured when she helped me to change Felix's nappy and sat next to him on the floor and played with him for a few minutes.

'When you come over tomorrow, it will be for the whole afternoon,' I told her. 'You can stay for tea and meet Amena, and I'll get you a taxi back to the hospital later on.'

I'd already told Amena what was happening and explained to her what a mother and baby placement was. I knew it was going to be a big change for her as well having another adult in the house, and it was important that she and Emily met before Emily moved in on Friday. I'd also told Emily about Amena.

'Amena might not be here for very long as she's due to leave soon,' I said.

'Is she being adopted?' Emily asked.

I explained that children came into the care system for different reasons, and I briefly touched on Amena's situation without giving away any confidential information.

'She and her mum are waiting for the council to find them some accommodation,' I told her. 'But there's such a lack of decent housing that it's taking a while.'

When Amena came home the next day, I introduced them.

'This is Felix's mum, Emily,' I told her. 'She's coming to stay with us from tomorrow.'

'Hi,' said Amena, giving Emily a shy smile. 'I love Felix. He's so cute.'

He was lying on his playmat so she went over and scooped him up and covered him with kisses.

'Let's play peekaboo,' she told him. 'He loves peekaboo doesn't he, Maggie?'

Amena put Felix on her knee and he giggled away as she covered her face with her hands and cried 'Peekaboo!'.

'And he likes it when I do this,' she smiled as she tipped Felix backwards and his mouth gaped open into a gummy grin.

Emily was watching them intently.

When Amena had gone upstairs, Emily was even quieter than usual. I knew it was going to be a big adjustment for her, living with me and Amena while she bonded with Felix and learnt more about his needs now he was older, but she looked so crestfallen. After a few minutes, she turned to me.

'So many people know more about my baby than me,' she admitted quietly. 'I'm just a stranger to him.'

I could see the sadness in her eyes.

'That's what the next few weeks are all about,' I told her. 'It's your chance to get to know Felix all over again. And you're certainly not a stranger to him.'

I explained that he would recognise her smell and the sound of her voice.

'Something will instinctively tell him that you're his mum,' I reassured her.

Once he had that continuity of care, he would know that she was the one who was there for him and they could develop their bond.

But Emily didn't say much more, and at dinner she pushed her food around her plate. Afterwards, Amena went upstairs to do her homework, leaving Emily and I time to chat.

'How have you found it?' I asked her. 'Can you believe that you're being discharged tomorrow?'

'It doesn't feel real,' she said. 'It's what I've wanted for so long but now it just feels scary.'

'There's no need for you to be scared,' I smiled. 'We're all here to support you.'

However, I knew the first week was going to be unsettling for us all as the dynamic in the house would change. It was going to be a particularly big adjustment for Emily as she was used to the regimented routine of the hospital. I desperately hoped that it wasn't too soon and that she was going to manage OK.

On Friday morning, Rupinder collected Emily from the hospital after she was discharged and drove her to my house. Emily looked shell-shocked.

'I can't believe it's actually happened,' she sighed. 'Part of me felt like I was going to be in there forever.'

'Onwards and upwards,' smiled Rupinder.

'Well, someone is very excited to see you,' I said, gesturing to a wriggling Felix in my arms.

I passed him to Emily and she took him, although I noticed that after a few minutes she put him down on the rug on the floor.

Rupinder said that one of the community mental health team would be calling round later to introduce themselves.

'At first, they'll visit every day or so to see how you're getting on, then they'll take it from there,' she said.

Emily's sessions at the family unit were due to start the following week as well.

When Rupinder left, I could see Emily felt awkward and didn't know what to do with herself.

'Why don't you go upstairs and unpack and get yourself settled?' I suggested.

'I haven't really got much,' she shrugged, gesturing to the holdall on the floor. 'Just a few things that the ward and the hospital social worker cobbled together for me.'

It gave me an idea.

'I'll have to run it by Rupinder, but why don't we go to your flat this weekend and you can pick up a few of your clothes and bits and pieces?'

She nodded.

I thought it might help her feel more settled if she had some of her own things around her.

Rupinder was fine with it, so the following day we put Felix in the car seat and Emily gave me directions. Her flat was in a converted Victorian school building.

'Wow, what a lovely building,' I said as we pulled into the car park.

Emily's flat was on the upper floor. I carried Felix and I was out of breath by the time we'd climbed two flights of stairs. Outside the front door, Emily suddenly hesitated as she was about to put the key in the lock.

'I know it must feel really strange being back here,' I said, putting a comforting hand on her arm.

She nodded and I could see that she was close to tears.

'It's OK,' I told her. 'We don't have to do this today. We can come back another time.'

I was cross with myself for not thinking this through properly and perhaps pushing her to do something that she wasn't ready for.

'No, I want to,' she nodded firmly. 'It's my home and I'll have to come back here sometime, so I may as well get it over with. And I want to get some of my clothes.'

'Well, I'm here with you and if it gets too much, we can leave,' I replied.

'Thank you,' she said.

Taking a deep breath, she turned the key in the lock, pushed the door open with her trembling hand, and we walked inside.

It had huge windows so the hallway was flooded with light and there were framed pictures all along the walls.

'What a lovely flat,' I told her.

As we walked through to the open-plan living room and kitchen, I gasped.

We both stopped dead in our tracks. I couldn't believe what I was seeing.

'I can't believe I did this,' gasped Emily. 'I'm so ashamed.'

Rupinder hadn't been joking all those weeks ago when she'd said that Emily had covered the walls in lists and notes. I'd assumed that she'd taken them down, but every inch of wall space was covered and they were everywhere. Most of them didn't make sense but a few did, and it was clear how much Emily's state of mind had deteriorated and how paranoid she'd been.

Emily looked as horrified as me as she stared at the walls.

'I'm so sorry,' she whispered, tearing up.

It wasn't just the walls either. All of the radiators and the TV were still covered with masking tape and bubble wrap.

Emily looked like she was going to collapse. 'I don't know what I was thinking writing these things.'

'Why don't you sit down for a minute?' I suggested.

I led her to the brown leather sofa, and she sat and sobbed.

'It's awful,' she wept. 'How could I say those terrible things about my own baby?'

A lot of the notes were about how Felix was evil, and the Devil, and how she thought he was going to hurt her.

I remembered how upset Rupinder had been when she'd come back from Emily's flat and, seeing it with my own eyes, I understood why now. When she'd OKed the visit, she'd obviously forgotten that the notes were still there otherwise I would have gone round beforehand and got rid of them myself.

All I could do was give Emily a hug.

'I can't believe I wrote all these things,' Emily sobbed. 'I'm the one who's evil, not Felix!'

'You were very poorly,' I said gently. 'That wasn't you talking, it was the illness.'

She shook her head.

'I got rid of all of his things,' she sighed. 'I remember being fixated on getting him adopted. I didn't want to see him again. How could I do that to my own baby? I don't deserve him.'

I looked at Felix who was fast asleep in his car seat on the floor.

'Emily, look at where you are now and remind yourself how far you've come,' I told her. 'You're so strong and you're working hard to get your son back. You've come such a long way and you should be so proud of yourself for that.'

'I'm not proud of any of this,' she sighed, gesturing to the walls. 'I feel so ashamed and so guilty that my son hasn't had a mother for the first few months of his life. I've let him down so badly.'

She started to sob again. I put my arms around her and let her cry it out. Slowly, she started to calm down.

'Do you want me to grab you some clothes and then we can go?' I asked her.

I was starting to regret coming here today and hoped it hadn't affected her recovery in a negative way.

Emily shook her head.

'No, I want to stay and get rid of all this,' she told me, pointing to the walls.

'OK,' I nodded.

If that was going to make her feel better then that's what we'd do. She told me where everything was, and I got some bin bags out from under the kitchen sink.

'Right,' I said. 'Let's do this.'

There was a satisfying ripping noise as I pulled five or six pages off the wall in one strip of tape. I screwed them into a ball and stuffed them into a bin bag.

'You see,' I said. 'Gone.'

Emily smiled through her tears. She stood up and headed to the other wall and did the same thing. Soon you could hardly hear anything except for the rip of tape and the scrunching of paper as we pulled pages and pages of Emily's notes, plans and ramblings off the walls and put them into the bin bags.

'It's very therapeutic,' I told her. 'But your walls are going to be a mess as the tape is pulling all the paint off too.'

'I don't care,' replied Emily. 'I want them gone. I'm trying not to read any of them.'

She started to pull the bubble wrap and masking tape off the radiator and the TV too.

Twenty minutes later, I was hot, sweaty and exhausted. We had filled four bin bags and the grey walls were a mess of tape marks and holes where we'd pulled the paint off as well as the tape.

'Don't worry,' I said. 'One of my neighbours is a painter and decorator and I'm sure we can get him to come in and give everything a quick coat of paint at some stage.'

'Thank you,' nodded Emily. 'And thank you for helping me.'

She looked upset again.

'I feel so guilty for everything I put Felix through,' she said, looking down at him. 'He was just a tiny baby. He needed me, but I let him down.'

'You were ill,' I told her.

Emily looked worried.

'What if I don't ever get over this?' she asked. 'What if I never go back to how I was?'

I could see the utter shame that she felt.

'You *will* get better,' I reassured her. 'Look how far you've come. You're back with Felix again and you're determined to prove yourself.'

I believed that Emily could do this and get better, but she needed to believe it too.

SIXTEEN

Facing the Fear

Slowly, we all started to settle into the new routine. The idea was that, with me there to support her, Emily would take over Felix's care.

To begin, we went back to basics as Emily admitted the first few weeks of Felix's life were a blur. I guided her through everything that she needed to do for him – how and when to give him a bottle, how often to change him, how to spot that he needed a nap or that he was teething. I'd talked her through giving him a bath then showed her how to settle him into his cot in my room for the night. Emily was expected to do everything connected to Felix. So at the end of the day, she'd sort out his washing, put his dirty nappies in the bin outside, tidy up his toys, sterilise his bottles and wipe down his playmat.

Once Felix was in bed, we'd sit down and talk about the day and how Emily thought things had gone, then we'd write my notes together before I sent them to Rupinder and Becky.

'Do we have to do this every night?' Emily asked wearily one evening.

'I'm afraid it's part of the assessment process,' I told her. 'But I think it's good for us to do it together so you can tell me how you think it's going and we can keep everyone updated and informed.'

However, I could see that Emily was exhausted by it all. She'd go to bed shortly after Felix did and I encouraged her to have a sleep when he napped at lunchtime too.

'Things will get easier as you adjust to life outside the hospital,' I reassured her.

In a way, her going to bed so early worked well as it gave me and Amena the chance to have some one-to-one time together so she didn't feel left out.

'How's it all going with Emily?' asked Rupinder in a phone call at the end of the first week.

'She's doing really well,' I told her. 'I only have to show her things once and she gets it. She's more than capable of looking after Felix and meeting his needs.'

Emily was an intelligent woman and it was clear that she could take responsibility for caring for her son.

'The workers at the family centre have said the same thing,' Rupinder told me. 'There doesn't seem to be any issue with the practicalities.'

I'd been dropping Emily and Felix off at the family centre for the two-hour sessions. As time went on, some of the sessions would just be Emily and the social workers and, on those occasions, Felix would stay at home with me.

A community mental health nurse was also calling in daily to see Emily. Unfortunately it wasn't always the same person, but a couple of times we'd had a woman in her thirties called

Kerry and I could tell Emily really liked and trusted her. I didn't sit in on their chats, but Kerry was there for support and to check that everything was OK with Emily's medication.

'Do you have any worries or concerns about Emily's mental health from what you've seen so far?' Rupinder asked me.

'Not at all,' I said. 'She seems to be doing really well in that respect too.'

Emily and I had agreed to be very open, and we talked about her mental health. She felt that her medication was working and that she was coping OK. She also hadn't suffered any delusions or paranoia.

Rupinder said the community mental health team and the family centre had both said the same thing.

'It sounds like things are going well so let's keep building on that,' Rupinder told me. 'I was thinking that maybe Emily could start having brief periods of time on her own with Felix? When he's having a nap then perhaps you could leave her on her own with him?' she suggested. 'Nothing major, just a few minutes at a time, with you elsewhere in the house.'

'We can definitely try that,' I replied.

In the kitchen one day, Felix had fallen asleep in his pram and Emily was sorting through some of his washing that she'd taken off the airer.

'I'm just going to pop upstairs to my bedroom,' I told her. 'Are you OK to stay here and keep an eye on Felix?'

Emily looked stunned.

'But I can't stay with him on my own,' she told me. 'That's not allowed.'

'It's OK,' I smiled. 'Rupinder said she was happy for you to start being on your own with him.'

Emily shook her head.

'No, I can't,' she told me. 'I need to go upstairs and put this washing away, then I've got some other things I need to do in my room.'

I thought she would have jumped at the chance to have some alone time with her son, even if he was asleep. However, I didn't want to rush things and I knew there would be plenty of other opportunities.

'That's OK,' I told her. 'You do what you need to do and I'll put the monitor on, then you'll hear him if he cries.'

A few days later, Felix fell asleep in his blow-up ring.

'Bless him,' I smiled. 'It's probably just a catnap as he had a sleep earlier. If it's OK with you, I'm just going to pop to the shop at the end of the road for some bread and a couple of pints of milk.'

'Why don't I go?' suggested Emily. 'I honestly don't mind.'

'No, you stay here with Felix,' I smiled. 'I could do with some fresh air and I'll be back in a few minutes.'

I grabbed my purse and headed out. The corner shop was at the end of my street. I got what I needed and, as I walked back up my road towards my house, I could see Emily at the front window with a worried look on her face.

I gave her a wave but she didn't wave back. By the time I walked up the path, the front door was wide open and Emily was there waiting for me. She looked ashen and I could see the panic in her eyes. My pulse started racing – had something happened to Felix?

'What is it, lovey?' I asked. 'Is the baby OK?'

'He's fine,' she mumbled. 'He's still asleep in the kitchen. You were ages. I was worried you weren't coming back.'

'Emily, I can't have been more than five minutes,' I told her.

She was pacing up and down now, wringing her hands, and she was struggling to breathe.

'Emily, what is it?' I asked. 'What's wrong?'

She started to cry and I could see her hands shaking as she brushed her tears away.

I led her into the kitchen, where thankfully Felix was still fast asleep, and we sat down on the sofa. I suspected that she was having a panic attack.

'You're OK,' I reassured her. 'Take some nice deep breaths. Felix is fine and you're fine.'

'I know,' she nodded. 'I know.'

However, I could see that she was still very jittery.

Thankfully, after a few minutes, her breathing start to slow and she began to calm down.

I put the kettle on and made us both a cup of tea. I suspected that Emily was doubting herself and I needed to give her a pep talk.

'I'm OK now,' she said, embarrassed, as I handed her a drink. 'I was just being silly.'

'It's not silly at all,' I reassured her. 'I just want you to know that everyone has been so impressed with how capable you are – so please don't question your abilities.'

She nodded.

'You're doing so well,' I told her. 'You can do this. In fact, if things carry on like this, I can talk to Rupinder about possibly moving Felix's cot into your room.'

I'd still need to have the baby monitor in my bedroom so I was aware of what was going on, but it would be a big step forward for Emily.

I thought she would be pleased but she looked absolutely horrified.

'What is it?' I asked her. 'I thought that was what you wanted?'

Emily shook her head and wouldn't look at me.

'No,' she said, her voice trembling. 'I can't do it, Maggie. He can stay in your room.'

Tears streamed down her face.

'Emily, you've got to talk to me about this,' I urged. 'Why wouldn't you want Felix to be in your room?'

'I just don't,' she snapped. 'I can't do it.'

'You've got to have faith in your own abilities,' I told her. 'I've seen for myself that you're more than capable of putting him to bed every night and settling him back to sleep if he wakes up.'

'It's not about that,' she replied. 'I just can't.'

'But why?' I asked.

'Because I'm scared of being on my own with him,' she told me. 'I can't do it. The thought terrifies me.'

Hearing her words was a shock.

'Oh, Emily,' I sighed. 'What is it that's scaring you?'

'I think when I'm on my own with him, it reminds me of how I felt all those months ago,' she told me. 'I think I might associate Felix with that dark time and it scares me that I might go back to that place again.'

'Oh, lovey,' I sighed, rubbing her back.

'What if it happens again and I have delusions or hallucinations and I want to hurt him or I think he's the devil like I wrote in all those notes?' she whimpered. 'I'm just so frightened. What if I had done something to hurt him?' she whispered.

'But you didn't,' I told her. 'And things are very different now. You're on medication and you've got a support network. We would all recognise the signs and there's a plan in place.'

I reminded Emily what Dr Pickard had told her.

'You *can* make a full recovery and there's no reason why this would happen again.'

'I want to believe you but I'm so scared,' she said. 'I'm fine when you or someone else is there with me, but when I'm on my own with Felix . . . I'm terrified. I can't do it, Maggie.'

She dissolved into tears again. It was awful to see her torturing herself, but I knew that unfortunately there was no quick fix.

'Please don't tell anyone about this,' she begged. 'I'm so ashamed to be scared of my own son.'

'Emily, I really wish I didn't have to, but I'm going to have to put this in my recordings and share our conversation with Rupinder,' I told her. 'It's something that we need to keep talking about.'

She looked worried.

'Do you think it would stop them from letting me have Felix?' she asked me.

I knew I needed to be honest with her about it.

'If it's something that you feel you can't overcome then yes,' I told her. 'If you're scared to be alone with your own baby, then that's a major problem.'

'I know, you're right,' she sniffed. 'But I'm trying so hard not to be.'

Rupinder and I had a chat about it when Emily was at the family centre the following day. I talked her through what had happened.

'I'm hopeful that in time she can overcome this,' I told her.

'She's going to need to,' replied Rupinder bluntly. 'If Emily can't be on her own with Felix then she's not going to be able to return home with him.'

I knew that Social Services weren't going to wait around forever. Even though they had every sympathy with Emily and what she'd been through, they were conscious of how old Felix was and his need to have a stable family life. If things weren't going to work out with Emily, then their priority would be to find him an adoptive family.

It was going to be a difficult conversation to have with Emily but one that I had to broach. She needed to know the reality of the situation.

'Did you talk to Rupinder about it?' she asked me.

'While everyone totally sympathises with what you've been through and acknowledges that your fear is understandable after that trauma, the reality is that Social Services won't wait forever,' I told her. 'For yours and Felix's sakes, you've got to try to move past this and move forward.'

Emily was still very tearful about it.

'I *am* trying,' she sobbed. 'I'm trying so hard, I promise.'

'I know you are,' I nodded. 'You can't change what happened. You can't change that you were ill. That wasn't in your control. But this is now in your control and you can acknowledge to yourself that you're scared but there's a lot of people around to support you – so you have to tell yourself that you can beat this and you can do it.'

Emily nodded.

'What will happen if I can't?' she asked.

'If you feel that you can't move past this fear, Social Services will want to start looking at other options for Felix while he's still young,' I told her. 'I know that's hard for you to hear but it's the reality.'

'I promise you, I'm going to try,' Emily told me. 'I can't let Felix down again.'

'Remember, we're all here to support you,' I told her. 'We all want this to work out for you both.'

I wanted Emily to be open with me about how she was feeling, and all we could do was to keep talking about her fear and keep hoping that it was something that she could overcome. There were long waiting lists but, at some stage, I was hoping that she would be able to access some counselling sessions.

One afternoon that week was lovely and sunny.

'Why don't you take Felix into the garden?' I suggested to Emily.

'But what would I do with him?' she asked anxiously.

'Just talk to him,' I suggested. 'Walk round with him in your arms and show him the flowers and the trees and talk to him about the colours or point out a bee or a butterfly.'

I opened the patio doors.

'It's nice and warm out there so I can leave the doors open,' I told her. 'I'll be right here and you'll be able to see me.'

I could see the fear in Emily's eyes.

'How about I set a timer on my phone?' I suggested.

That way, at least she'd know what she was dealing with and it would perhaps make being alone with Felix seem more manageable.

I showed her the timer that I'd set for five minutes.

'It's just five minutes,' I told her. 'And I'll be here for reassurance.'

'OK,' she nodded.

As I passed Felix to her, I could see how hesitant she was.

'You can do this,' I smiled, pressing 'start' on the timer.

I watched from the window as Emily walked around the garden with Felix. She didn't say much to him at first and kept glancing back to the kitchen window where I was stood washing up. I gave her a supportive smile.

Kerry, the mental health nurse, had talked Emily through a few techniques to try if she felt panicky and I could tell that she was now trying to control her breathing.

Please let her be able to do this, I thought. Not only would it give her a much-needed boost, but if she couldn't spend five minutes alone with her son, we were in trouble. The next time I looked up, I could see Emily was chatting to Felix and he was reaching out to grab a flower.

Suddenly, the timer went off, disturbing my thoughts, and Emily hurried inside. She immediately put Felix down on the floor.

'How was that?' I asked.

'It was OK,' she shrugged. 'I really had to fight the urge to come back in.'

'But you didn't,' I smiled. 'You got through it.'

'I think Felix liked it,' she told me. 'He was reaching out and trying to touch all the flowers.'

It was such a small pocket of time but it felt like a huge milestone for Emily.

'Well done,' I told her. 'I'm so proud of you.'

It was good that she'd acknowledged her fear, and hopefully it would lessen the more time she spent on her own with Felix. I didn't expect things to suddenly change overnight – it was about slowly moving forward. If Emily could prove that she was making progress then it would be OK. I knew it was a case of taking baby steps and getting Emily to face her fears with my support.

A few days later, she managed five minutes on her own with Felix in the living room. We used the timer again to break it down into a manageable chunk. I could see that it was still terrifying for her and it didn't feel normal or natural, but I was hopeful that we would get there.

'Remember how you were scared to even hold Felix at first in the hospital?' I reminded her.

She nodded.

'But in the end, you got there.'

'I bet people think I'm so stupid and pathetic,' she sighed. 'I'm too scared to be with my own son.'

'Most people haven't been through what you have or overcome what you've faced,' I told her. 'I know it all feels overwhelming right now, but you can do this.'

SEVENTEEN

Hope

Beads of sweat dripped down Charlie's forehead as he turned the Allen key in the final bolt.

'There you go,' he nodded. 'All done.'

'Thank you so much,' I told him as we walked onto the landing. 'I really appreciate this.'

'Emily, come and have a look,' I yelled downstairs.

We all trooped into Emily's bedroom, where Charlie had kindly put up Edie's old cot. He and Louisa had offered to lend it to us as Edie now had a toddler bed and hadn't slept in the cot for a good year.

It meant we had two cots for Felix – one in my room and one in Emily's. The aim was that Emily would slowly get used to having Felix in her bedroom and hopefully build up to feeling comfortable enough to have him with her for the whole night.

'How do you feel about seeing the cot in your room?' I asked her when Charlie had gone.

'Scared,' she said. 'Nervous.'

Things had been slowly getting easier over the last few weeks and Emily's fears around Felix were lessening, however it was taking time. I felt that having two cots would ease the pressure somehow. Rather than moving his cot from my room to hers, we could do it at her own pace.

'Do you want to try putting Felix down for his nap in the cot in your room?' I suggested at lunchtime.

'OK,' she nodded.

As this was the first time, I stayed in the bedroom with her so she felt supported. We'd already put Felix's elephant blanket and his fluffy rabbit in the cot and his eyes grew heavy as soon as Emily gently lowered him down onto the mattress.

'Are you going to come downstairs or are you going to stay up here with him?' I asked her, as she normally liked to sleep when Felix had his nap.

'No, I'll come down with you,' she said quickly.

I could sense her panic and I didn't want to push her too far, too soon. So we put the baby monitor on and went downstairs.

A few days later, I decided to try to move things along a bit.

'I'm going to wait at the top of the stairs while you put Felix down on your own,' I told Emily.

The bedroom door was wide open so she felt more secure.

'You know what you're doing but I'm right here,' I smiled.

'Thanks,' she nodded. I could see she was wary, but the fact she didn't question my suggestion was a step in the right direction.

A couple of days later, I switched things up again and told Emily I was going to wait at the bottom of the stairs this time while she put Felix down for his nap.

'You'll be absolutely fine,' I said. 'But shout if you need me.'

'OK,' she said, with more strength in her voice this time.

I could see that although her fear around being alone with Felix was easing, it hadn't entirely gone yet. But, as I'd told Rupinder, things were definitely moving in the right direction and Emily was still willing to keep working at it.

This lunchtime, however, Felix was not happy about being put down for his nap. I could hear him crying and thrashing around.

'Are you OK?' I called up to Emily.

She came to the bedroom door.

'He's not happy,' she told me. 'I'm just going to sit with him for a bit and see if he settles.'

'OK, flower,' I nodded. 'If you need any help, give me a shout.'

While it wasn't great that Felix was refusing his nap, in my head I felt like cheering. It showed how far Emily had come in the past few weeks that she was even prepared to be alone in the same room as her son. Half an hour later, she came down holding an exhausted-looking Felix. She was close to tears.

'I really tried,' she sighed. 'But no matter what I did, he just wouldn't sleep so I gave up. Maybe I wasn't doing it right, or he wanted you and not me?'

Emily still wasn't confident in her abilities as a mother and was always quick to blame herself.

'Please don't worry about it,' I reassured her. 'He's done the same to me so many times before. Maybe he's teething again as his cheeks are all red? Remember no one expects you to be perfect. Babies have a mind of their own and often it's not related to anything that you're doing or not doing.'

★

A few days later, we had an appointment to see the health visitor so Felix could have a check-up. It was a good way to engage Emily and encourage her to feel like she was fully involved in his development.

There was a baby weigh-in clinic that morning so the wating room was packed full of mums with babies. Most of them were newborns and, at almost six months, Felix looked like a giant in comparison.

We managed to squeeze past all the prams and find a couple of spare seats. I knew Emily often found 'official' things like this overwhelming.

'Don't worry,' I smiled. 'It's not a test. Just a quick check-up. Remember, no one's trying to catch you out or is judging you.'

I knew she always felt so ashamed when the health visitor read her notes and learnt about her background and that Felix was in foster care.

As we sat and waited, I couldn't help but overhear two mums next to us talking.

'Guess what?' one of them said to the other. 'She smiled for the first time yesterday.'

'Aw, that's adorable,' sighed the other mum. 'I can't wait for him to start doing that. It makes all those sleepless nights worth it.'

'I couldn't believe it,' she gasped. 'Honestly, it melted my heart. I took about a million photos and now I spend every waking minute trying to get her to do it again.'

I could see Emily listening to them intently.

'I'm just going to go to the loo,' she told me.

When she'd been gone ten minutes I thought I'd better check on her.

Emily was hunched over one of the sinks, splashing her eyes with water. I could tell that she'd been crying.

'What is it?' I asked.

'I was listening to those mums talking about their babies smiling and it brought it home to me all those moments I missed out on with Felix,' she sniffed. 'All of those milestones that I wasn't there to see and I'll never get back.'

'There are so many more milestones to come that you'll hopefully be there for,' I reassured her. 'It's such a tiny part of his life. Felix won't remember.'

'But I will,' nodded Emily. 'That awful realisation of what I did is the last thing I think about at night and the first thing that I remember every morning when I wake up.'

'You have to forgive yourself and try to move on from it,' I told her. 'You can't let it destroy you.'

But Emily wasn't sure that she could.

'Why did it happen to me, Maggie?' she sighed. 'What did I do wrong to deserve it?'

A lot of her upset was now turning to anger.

'I'd wanted to have a baby for so long and I was so happy to be pregnant,' she continued. 'It's so unfair. It was supposed to be such a special time.'

'I know,' I nodded. 'It's so unfair and I don't have any answers but you can't blame yourself. It wasn't your fault.'

Emily nodded.

'All the doctors and the mental health nurses and the social workers tell me that,' she sighed. 'But at the end of the day, I missed out on so much and I'm so scared that Felix will never truly bond with me.'

'Bonding is an ongoing process,' I told her. 'It doesn't just happen in the first few weeks of a baby's life. Every day you're bonding with him more and more.'

I reminded her how Felix would instinctively know that she was his mummy.

'Do you really believe that or are you just saying that to make me feel better?' she sighed.

'No, I really believe it,' I told her. 'I've read studies on it too. It's almost like muscle memory. I believe there's something innate within Felix that tells him you're his mum. And even though you were apart from each other for several months, he will still remember and recognise the sound of your voice, your smell and your touch.'

That night, I was talking things through with Vicky. It always felt good to get someone else's point of view who wasn't closely involved with the child.

'Poor love,' she sighed when I told her how Emily was struggling. 'She's really been through it.'

'I have no worries about her being able to look after Felix well,' I told her. 'But I do feel like there's an element of going through the motions rather than really connecting with him.'

It was as much about building up Emily's self-confidence and self-belief as it was about her building a bond with Felix.

'You can't rush these things,' Vicky told me. 'It will either come naturally or she's just not ready.'

I knew she was right, but I was so desperate to help Emily and for her to prove to Social Services that she could do this.

I knew that physical touch was a good way of encouraging that bond, so I showed Emily how to give Felix a massage after his bath with some baby cream. However, he was rolling all over the place and kept flipping himself off the playmat.

'He's so wriggly,' she laughed. 'I feel like I'm in a wrestling match.'

At least it had made her smile.

I knew it was also about not being afraid to be silly around him.

'He loves it when Amena reads him this board book and makes all the animal noises,' I told her. 'Why don't you give it a go?'

'You and Amena are so good at stuff like that,' Emily said. 'I just feel stupid.'

But after his bath that night, she put Felix on her knee.

'"Mooo" goes the cow,' she told him.

Felix looked at her intently with a confused look on his face. But Emily refused to give up.

'Then along came the dog,' she told him. '"Woof woof" went the doggy.'

This time Felix looked up at her and broke into the biggest grin. Fuelled by her success, Emily did a very loud impression of a chicken clucking.

Felix nearly jumped out of his skin and then gave a big chuckle.

Hearing him giggle made our hearts melt and soon Emily and I were laughing along too.

'You were right,' she beamed. 'He loves it.'

I suddenly realised that the best encouragement was going to come from Felix and not me. He was doing my job for me. With his actions, he was telling Emily that what she was doing was right and that she was his mummy – and that was all she needed.

I could see how proud she was of herself and it was heartwarming to see her smiling so happily too.

'I never realised that I had a hidden talent for animal impressions,' she giggled.

One afternoon, Emily had a solo session at the family centre so I looked after Felix. By the time Amena came home from being out with Hodan, I was tearing my hair out.

'I don't know what's got into Felix today,' I told her. 'He's really crotchety and restless, and he hasn't had a single nap.'

Amena offered to take him for a bit but he was very whiny with her as well.

Just before 5 p.m., Emily got back from the family centre. She looked exhausted as she flopped down next to Amena and Felix on the sofa.

As she was telling us about her session, Felix was straining towards her and holding his arms out.

'I think he wants his mummy,' said Amena.

Emily looked surprised.

'You mean me?' she asked.

'Well, I can't see any other mummies around here,' I laughed.

Felix leant over to her and Emily scooped him up.

'He's been a little monkey all afternoon,' I told her. 'He's been so unsettled. I just don't know what's wrong with him.'

I made us all a decaf coffee and when I turned back with the mugs, Felix was fast asleep in Emily's arms.

'Now that's better,' I smiled. 'He looks so peaceful.'

'Maybe that's what was wrong all along?' suggested Amena. 'He just wanted his mummy.'

'I think you're right,' I said. 'Felix certainly knows who he wants.'

Emily sat there with a contented smile on her face.

It was all about showing her that she could bond with Felix and that there was nothing to be scared of.

Later that evening, Emily came to me.

'I'd really like it if Felix was allowed to stay in my room with me tonight,' she said.

I was taken aback.

'Of course he can, but are you sure?' I asked her. 'I don't want you to feel pressured into it and he has been pretty unsettled all day.'

'No, I want him to,' she nodded. 'I want to go to bed and see him lying next to me. I feel like it's time.'

I suggested putting the baby monitor in my room just in case.

'Thank you,' she said. 'That's really reassuring.'

Emily said she was going to go to bed when Felix did. Half an hour later, I went to check on them. Peeping through the gap in the door, I could see Felix lying on his back in the cot with Emily in the single bed next to him. They were both fast asleep and I could see Felix's chest rise and fall. His little chubby fist was poking through the cot bars and Emily's hand was clutching onto it.

I smiled to myself. At last, it felt like we were making real progress.

EIGHTEEN

Leaving the Past Behind

With fostering, the one constant was that there was always change on the horizon and the dynamic in my house was about to shift once again. It started with a call from Amena's social worker, Rachel.

'I've got some great news,' she told me.

She explained that, after weeks of waiting, a property had finally come up for Hodan and Amena. It sounded perfect – it was a brand-new, two-bedroom house owned by a housing association.

'There's one catch,' added Rachel.

It was in a town an hour and a half's drive away, which meant Amena would have to move to study for her A levels at a different college closer to their new home.

'Hodan's keen to go for it,' Rachel told me. 'And if she wants to secure it, she has to sign for it in the next couple of days. She desperately wants to be with her daughter again, and you and I both know there's a shortage of decent housing.'

'I completely understand,' I said.

Rachel was going to come round and talk to Amena about it. As her social worker, she wanted to make sure that moving to another town to live with her mum was what Amena genuinely wanted to do. As she was almost seventeen now, her views had to be taken into consideration and there were other options open to her, such as staying with me or going into independent living.

When Rachel told Amena the news, she looked elated at first and then disappointed when told where their new home would be.

'I'm afraid it would mean moving to a different college than where you had planned to go to,' Rachel told her.

Rachel offered her time to think about it but Amena said that she didn't need to.

'I want to be with my mum,' she nodded. 'I'll be sad to leave my friends and Maggie, but I want to live with Mum again and she needs to get out of that hostel.'

Their bond was so strong, I knew she was prepared to give everything up to be with her.

I was really proud of Amena although I knew I was going to miss her terribly. There wasn't much time to get used to the idea either, as the plan was for them to move in less than a week.

There was one thing that I wanted to do before Amena left – I wanted to take her out for a meal on our own. Over the past few weeks she'd been spending so much time with Hodan, and I'd been so focused on Emily and Felix, that I felt like I'd hardly seen her. I wanted to catch up with her on her own and check she was OK. It was my way of saying goodbye to her. It was also a good test for Emily to be left on her own with Felix.

'Are you sure that's OK?' I asked Emily.

I explained that we were only going to go for a quick pizza at a local restaurant.

'If you want, I can ask Louisa or Vicky to come and sit with you while I'm gone?' I told her.

'No, I'll be absolutely fine,' she said.

We were over halfway through the mother and baby placement, and things were continuing to go well. Felix was sleeping in Emily's room permanently now and she was coping well, so being on her own with Felix for a couple of hours didn't seem to faze her.

It allowed me the opportunity for some much-treasured time with Amena.

'All the time I've been living with you I don't think we've been on our own that much,' she smiled. 'And I don't think you've ever taken me out for a pizza.'

'Well, I wanted to give you a special goodbye,' I told her. 'And I wanted you to know that you can come back and see us whenever you want and come for a sleepover.'

'That would be cool,' she nodded. 'I'm really going to miss you and Felix.'

I'd also arranged to have a little goodbye tea party at my house. Vicky and Paige were going to come, as well as Louisa and Edie and Charlie if he could finish work on time. Rachel was also going to pop in along with my supervising social worker, Becky.

I talked Emily through what was happening.

'I know it might be a bit overwhelming, so I understand if you want to disappear up to your bedroom,' I told her. 'However, Amena is really fond of Felix and people will want to see him and give him a cuddle – I wanted to make sure it's all OK with you.'

'That's fine,' she nodded.

It ended up being a really lovely afternoon, although I could see Emily was struggling, so I wasn't surprised when, after fifteen minutes, she told me she was going up to her room.

'Are you happy for Felix to stay down here with me?' I asked her.

'Yes, of course,' she nodded. 'I just don't think I'm up to socialising yet.'

I completely understood. She was currently having her medication reviewed to see if she could go on a different dose or combination that would make her less exhausted in the afternoons.

Everyone had made such an effort for Amena's tea party. Vicky and Louisa had baked a cake and Becky had brought a giant cookie with 'Good Luck' piped on it in icing. It all felt so final and so quick.

'I haven't got you a present,' I told Amena. 'But I want you to take anything you'd like from your room here that might work for your bedroom at the new house.'

I knew Hodan and Amena didn't have much stuff from their old flat and there wouldn't be any spare cash for furniture or décor, and I wanted Amena to feel comfortable and settled.

Social Services had arranged a moving van, so I was happy for her to take the rug and lamps and anything else that she thought she and Hodan might need.

By the time Amena went to bed for the last time in my house a few days later, her room looked so bare as everything was packed up and sitting in the hall, ready for the van tomorrow.

'It feels so strange and echoey in here,' I said.

'It's going to feel even stranger not living here anymore,' Amena told me, her voice quivering. 'I know you don't like to get sad when kids go, Maggie, but I do feel really sad about it.'

She'd had a tearful goodbye with her friends that day, and they had made her a special photo album.

'I feel sad too,' I smiled, squeezing her hand. 'And that's OK. But I'm really happy for you as well. I know how excited your mum is to have you back again and you're going to be so happy in your lovely new home and you'll make lots of friends when you start at your new college.'

The following morning, Hodan came to pick Amena up in a taxi. I stood on the pavement and gave Amena a big hug.

'I'm going to miss you, but come and visit whenever you want,' I reminded her.

Emily stood at the window with Felix, and Amena blew him a kiss.

'Felix is going to be really big the next time I see him,' she sighed.

In my head, I thought that if things went to plan, Felix was hopefully not going to be living here the next time that Amena came back to visit.

As I waved Hodan and Amena off, I felt that familiar stab of grief that came with seeing another child leave my home. It was particularly hard with Amena as I'd grown so fond of her and she'd been good company. However, I knew that lingering feeling of sadness would eventually ease and I had other things to focus on – such as the outcome of Emily and Felix's mother and baby placement.

Rupinder and I had regular catch-ups about it.

'The main aim now is to make sure that Emily can cope with Felix in the real world,' she told me on our last call.

It was all about encouraging her to do normal things with him that she would do in everyday life. Everyone was on board with it: the family centre encouraged Emily to get the bus there with Felix in place of relying on a lift or taxi, and instead of coming to my house, Kerry, the mental health nurse, would arrange for Emily to meet her in the park for a walk. They were all little but important tasks that encouraged Emily to take responsibility for her baby. She now did all the shopping for Felix too.

As Felix was six months old, Emily started to focus on weaning him. She'd realised that giving him his first taste of food was one milestone she was going to experience, and she had thrown herself into it with gusto. She'd read all the books and spent the past few weeks puréeing every fruit and vegetable she could get her hands on. My freezer was now full of ice-cube trays of pulped carrots, apples and courgettes.

She was determined to do everything by the book and give Felix his first taste of food.

'I'm going to give him carrots to begin with, so he doesn't get used to the sweet taste of fruit first,' she told me.

That morning, she carefully defrosted a couple of cubes of puréed carrot while Felix sat in the highchair with the new bowl, bibs and spoons that she'd bought him.

'Here you go,' she smiled, pushing the plastic spoon of carrot into his mouth.

She watched excitedly and had me take a photo as Felix licked the spoon suspiciously.

'He had a little bit!' she told me.

He moved the carrot around a couple of times in his mouth and then spat it straight out.

Emily looked crestfallen.

She tried another spoonful but he did exactly the same thing.

'Did I do it wrong?' she asked me. 'Maybe it was too cold or should I have given him apple instead?'

'Don't be too hard on yourself,' I told her. 'Babies never do what you want them to do or stick to the plan. Some babies are just not interested in food at first.'

I didn't want her to put too much pressure on herself and then feel like a failure. However, I could see that she wanted to do things right and I admired her determination and focus.

I also thought it would be good for her to try to socialise with other parents, so I encouraged her to go to a mother and baby group at the local church hall.

'It might be nice for you to meet other mums and build up a bit of a support network,' I suggested.

It was another ordinary, everyday thing. However, fifteen minutes later, Emily was stood on the doorstep in tears.

My heart sank.

'What on earth happened?' I asked her.

'I couldn't do it,' she sighed. 'They were talking about crawling and leaky nappies and baby swimming lessons, and I just froze and panicked.

'I can't have those conversations,' she sighed. 'I don't know how.'

She explained that she'd felt like she was going to have a panic attack.

'What if they'd asked me a question about when Felix was a newborn? I just don't know what to say.'

I felt so sorry for her.

'You don't have to tell them if you don't want to,' I said. 'They don't know anything about what you've been through.'

'But I feel like a fraud,' sighed Emily. 'I feel so different to them. While they were breastfeeding and watching *Homes Under the Hammer,* I was psychotic and abandoning my baby at the train station. They probably read about Felix in the paper.'

I tried to reassure her.

'I'm sorry for pushing it,' I told her. 'I thought it might be nice for you to connect with other people.'

I suggested that taking Felix to do an activity might be better, so there was a focus and she had something to do rather than feeling the pressure of having to sit around and chat.

'What sort of activity?' she asked.

'There are so many groups,' I told her. 'Things like sensory play or music groups or story times.'

I offered to look a few up for her.

I knew that Emily had recently been thinking a lot about those early days after Felix was born. She'd been talking about it with the community mental health team and she'd been doing some work around it at the family centre.

I tried to be as open as I could with her and encourage her to talk about it.

'Do you remember much about those first few weeks after Felix was born?' I asked her.

She shook her head.

'All I remember is that awful feeling of despair and how terrified I was.'

She explained that Dr Pickard had gone over it all with her when she was in hospital.

'I was horrified by the things I'd done and said,' she sighed. 'It was like Dr Pickard was talking about a different person and I don't honestly think I'll ever get over that. The shame will stay with me for the rest of my life.'

'They were symptoms of the illness – that wasn't you,' I said to her.

No matter how many times I told her, I wondered when she would truly start to believe it. And if she couldn't, would she ever truly be able to move on with Felix and put the past behind her?

NINETEEN

Lucky

We were now eight weeks into the ten-week mother and baby placement and I could see that Emily was getting impatient.

'When will they decide if I can have custody of Felix?' she sighed. 'I keep asking the workers at the family centre and Rupinder, but all they keep saying to me is that I'm doing really well.'

'Well, it's true,' I smiled.

'But I need some answers,' she told me.

I could see how frustrated she was.

'Why don't I ask Rupinder to pop round for a cup of tea one afternoon and we can all chat about the last few weeks of the placement and what the expectations are?'

'If you think that would help,' Emily said. 'Everything just feels so uncertain.'

In a way, it was a good sign that she was frustrated as it meant that she wanted to make plans to move forward and that she'd started thinking about the future.

The following afternoon, Rupinder came to see her.

'I know it must feel like everything is up in the air but there's not a lot more I can say at this stage,' Rupinder told her. 'The feedback is very positive.'

'That's all anyone is saying to me,' Emily sighed.

Over the past few weeks, slowly but surely, I'd been taking big backward steps until Emily had completely taken over everything connected to Felix. She decided when and what he ate, when he napped, what he wore and what they did in their spare time. I had very little involvement apart from sneaking in the odd cuddle from time to time, reading him a story or having a quick play if Emily needed to do something.

'Over these next couple of weeks, it's about moving the assessment on,' Rupinder told her. 'So, we want to see you and Felix together at your flat and see how you cope with him in your own home environment.'

Rather than go to the family centre now, one of the workers would meet Emily at her flat and spend some time with her there.

After Rupinder had left, I could see Emily was deep in thought.

'I can't bear going back to that flat like it was,' she sighed. 'Everything reminds me of being ill and I'm worried that all the old feelings might start to creep back.'

I could understand that she wanted a fresh start. She didn't want to walk back into her flat and be reminded of everything that had happened over the past six months. She owned the property so she couldn't just move out.

'I need to redecorate,' she said decisively. 'Maggie, will you help me?'

'Of course,' I said. 'And I know a good decorator I can put you in touch with.'

Emily still had some savings leftover from her maternity leave, so we took Felix into town one day and she chose some paint colours.

'I think I'm going to wallpaper the sitting room,' she said. 'I want it to look and feel really different. I want to redo Felix's room too, and I'll have to buy another cot and some drawers to replace the things I gave away.'

Hearing her talk about redecorating Felix's room made me feel slightly uneasy – Emily was doing all of this before we knew the final outcome of the assessment. *She* would be going back to her flat but, the reality was, we didn't know at this stage if Felix was going back to live with her too. I was worried that she was getting too far ahead of herself.

However, I decided to keep my concerns to myself. It was nice to see Emily so positive, and wanting to decorate Felix's room and make plans for him and their life together. I just hoped that she would get to take her baby home.

Please let it be OK, I said to myself.

But I knew how quickly things could suddenly change with an assessment, particularly where mental health was concerned. When I'd read up about postpartum psychosis after Emily's diagnosis, I'd seen that it wasn't unusual for a mother to have a relapse a few months later or to suffer from depression. Over the years, I had seen many assessments break down in the last few weeks for one reason or another. I wanted to stay positive for Emily but I knew that, at this stage, nothing was certain. She just had to keep moving forward and demonstrating her commitment to Felix.

Thankfully their bond had continued to grow. Now when I held him, he looked around for his mum and if he spotted Emily, he leant towards her and held out his arms.

In the penultimate week of the placement, Emily was going to meet a worker from the family centre at her flat and then stay there for the afternoon on her own with Felix.

I dropped her off and came in for half an hour, then went back later to pick her up.

'How did it feel being back home with Felix?' I asked.

'I don't know,' she said, shaking her head a little. 'It felt very normal actually.'

Emily said the worker had been talking to her about her long-term plans.

'She was asking me about my job in finance and if I intended to go back.'

'Do you feel like you'd like to go back to work one day?' I asked her.

'I think I will have to,' she nodded. 'Maybe not right away and not full-time, but I love my job.'

Her employer had suggested that she go into her office to talk to them about her plans following her parental leave. She'd emailed her boss and set up a meeting for in a few days' time.

On the morning of the meeting, I could tell that Emily was nervous. She changed her outfit two or three times, but she'd finally settled on some wide-leg trousers, a stripy shirt and some loafers. She'd straightened her hair and put make-up on.

'You look very professional,' I smiled.

'I really wish I felt like that,' she sighed. 'I'm so scared.'

'You've got nothing to be nervous about,' I reassured her.

However, I could see that all-too-familiar fear was creeping back in.

'I'm so ashamed and embarrassed,' she sighed. 'Everyone at work knows what happened to me because the police went to talk to them after I was arrested. I'm mortified that they all know what I did.'

We'd talked a lot about the shame that Emily still clearly felt.

'Remember you're recovering from a serious illness,' I told her. 'Everyone knows that you were very unwell. You wouldn't be feeling this way if you were going back to work after recovering from an operation, would you?'

Even though things had come a long way, there was still such a stigma around mental health.

I looked after Felix while Emily went into the office to talk to her boss and HR. When she arrived back two hours later, I could tell that the meeting had gone well.

'Everyone was so nice,' she smiled. 'They're going to keep my job open for me until I'm ready to come back and they said they're happy for me to go part-time.'

'That's wonderful news,' I told her.

Emily described how she'd got emotional when she'd walked into the office.

'The last time I was there, I was heavily pregnant and so excited to meet my baby boy,' she told me. 'How did it all go so wrong, Maggie?'

I gave her a hug and she cried quietly in my arms.

With my encouragement, Emily had recently started taking Felix to a local baby sensory class once a week. She'd been nervous the first few times and I'd had to talk her into going, but she was starting to enjoy it.

'Felix loves it, so I make myself do it for him,' she told me.

'I'm really proud that you're forcing yourself out of your comfort zone,' I told her.

The last few times she'd gone, she'd even got chatting to one of the other mums. Emily explained that Esther had two daughters – a one-year-old called Lola and an older daughter, Eliza, who was six and at school. Esther had invited her out for a coffee after this week's class.

'I'm not sure whether I'll go,' Emily said, looking nervous. 'You know how social things make me uncomfortable.'

However, she came back a couple of hours later, beaming.

'Guess what, Maggie?' she told me. 'Esther had it too.'

She explained that when they'd got chatting, Esther had told her how she'd had postpartum psychosis after the birth of her eldest daughter.

'It got really bad within days of her being born,' she told me. 'She didn't sleep for a week as she thought her husband was going to kill the baby.'

She'd ended up spending three months in a mother and baby unit.

'Poor woman,' I sighed. 'How is she now?'

'She's fully recovered,' nodded Emily. 'It didn't come back when she had Lola and she's not on any medication anymore.'

Emily said she'd told Esther about her own experience, and I could see how much it had helped her to talk to someone who had been through something similar and had come out the other side.

'She knew exactly what it was like,' Emily told me. 'It made me feel better to know that you can get over it and hopefully come out of it as a stronger person.'

Esther had told her about a postpartum psychosis support group that met once a month.

'It's an hour's drive away but Esther goes, and she said the next time there's a meeting then we can go together.'

'I think that's a great idea,' I smiled.

I could see that hearing about Esther's experiences had made Emily feel less alone, and that's exactly what she needed right now.

With ten days left of the placement, Rupinder organised another LAC review.

'Is it OK to have it at your house again?' she asked me.

I was happy to host it as I thought it would make it more relaxed and informal for Emily. She hadn't attended the last one, but this time she was determined to be there. I could tell that she was nervous about the review and I talked her through who would be there and what was likely to happen.

'This is where they're probably going to make a decision about Felix's long-term future,' I told her.

'But who decides what's going to happen to him?' she asked.

'They'll go around the room and everyone will give their opinion, and we'll make a collective decision,' I said. 'Everyone has to be in agreement on what's the best way forward for Felix.'

I explained that Felix's IRO, Peter, would probably lead things. His role was to chair the meeting and make sure that any decision made was in Felix's best interests.

'You'll already know everyone else there,' I told her.

Rupinder would be present, as well as someone from the family centre, and hopefully Kerry, Emily's community mental health nurse, and my supervising social worker, Becky.

'Sometimes they ask a health visitor to come along too,' I told her.

On the morning of the review, I could see Emily was struggling.

'I didn't sleep a wink last night and I feel sick,' she sighed. 'I'm dreading what they're going to say.'

She sat in the living room, clinging onto Felix.

As everyone arrived and chit-chatted about the weather and Becky got us all a glass of water, Emily leant over to me.

'I don't think I can do this,' she whispered.

She looked ashen and I could see her whole body was trembling.

'It's going to be OK,' I told her, giving her hand a squeeze.

Peter opened the meeting and introduced everyone. Kerry was the first to speak.

'Emily has really been through it,' she sighed. 'Postpartum psychosis is rare and terrifying, and Emily has really had to fight hard to overcome it.'

She looked over at Emily and smiled. 'It's been very tough for her and she has struggled at times, especially when it's come to establishing a bond with Felix. But she's always been very open with us about how she's feeling and slowly, she's become stronger.'

Kerry discussed how the medication was continuing to work well and that Emily hadn't suffered any further psychosis or delusions.

I could see Emily was listening intently.

Rupinder echoed Kerry's sentiments.

'Emily has really struggled, but she's tried so hard and she's established a really good relationship with Felix now,' she nodded. 'And I have no concerns at all about the way that she cares for him.'

Rupinder turned to me.

'What are your thoughts, Maggie?' she asked. 'Out of everyone here today, you're probably the one who knows Emily and Felix best.'

Emily looked at me nervously.

'Emily has been to hell and back,' I said. 'What should have been the happiest time of her life turned into her worst nightmare. But I've been so impressed by her dedication and focus to try to get better for Felix. She's fought for that bond with him and, as you can see, he knows who his mummy is.'

Everyone smiled as they looked at Felix, who was now fast asleep on Emily's knee.

Margaret from the family centre agreed with everything the rest of us had said.

'And is there anything that you want to say, Emily?' Peter asked her.

She nodded and I gave her trembling hand a supportive squeeze.

'I just want to say thank you to everyone for all you've done for me,' she said in a quiet voice. 'It's been the hardest thing that I've ever faced in my life, and I think it's something that's always going to be with me and that has changed me irrevocably as a person.

'But I can assure you that I've worked very hard to prove that this isn't going to beat me. I love my son so much and I will fight with everything in me to give him the best life that I can . . .'

Her voice started to quiver.

'I want to reassure you that that person who abandoned her newborn at the train station wasn't really me. That was a very sick woman and I'll do everything in my power to make sure that woman never comes back again.'

She took a deep breath and clutched Felix a little tighter.

'So I'm begging all of you, please let my son come back to where he belongs with me, his mummy. Please give us a chance to be a family again.'

I felt a lump form in my throat and I looked across at Rupinder, who was wiping away a tear.

'All I can say is thank you, Emily,' said Peter. 'It's clear to everyone here the love that you have for your son and how dedicated you have been to work through every challenge and obstacle.

'Reading everyone's reports, all I can see are positives. I know it hasn't been easy but you've more than proved yourself as capable of looking after Felix. You've made remarkable progress and I know everyone agrees that the best outcome for Felix is to return him back to your care full-time.'

We all nodded and smiled while Emily stared at us, stunned. I felt a sense of relief wash over me.

'All that's left to say is I wish you both every luck for the future,' Peter told her.

Emily looked like she was struggling to take it all in.

'Well done,' I told her. 'I'm so proud of you!'

'I can't believe it,' she gasped. 'I've got my baby back!'

Before he closed the meeting, Peter ran through the ongoing support that Emily would continue to have once she and Felix moved back home. The community mental health team would see her once or twice a week to start off with and Rupinder would be checking in with her weekly too.

'We're not going to leave you on your own,' she smiled.

After everyone else had gone, Emily, Rupinder and I sat down together and worked out how the next few days were going to go.

'It's up to you when you move back to the flat,' Rupinder told her.

'I think I need another few days just to get everything ready for Felix – then we're good to go,' smiled Emily.

Rupinder thought it would be advisable for Emily and Felix to sleep over at the flat together for a night before they moved back home permanently.

'I think that would be good to boost your confidence and check there are no issues,' she suggested. 'If that goes well then there's no reason why Felix can't be home with you by the weekend.'

'Wow,' Emily gasped. 'I still can't take it in.'

I could see the review had left Emily absolutely shattered but she threw herself into making plans. Every day when she went to the flat to sort out furniture deliveries or let tradespeople in, she took Felix with her.

A couple of days after the LAC review, she was planning to stay overnight.

'If there are any issues at all then give me a ring,' I told her.

I knew she was more than capable of looking after Felix, but I was still on edge.

I lay in bed that night, wondering how it was all going. When my phone beeped with a text, I leapt on it.

All fine here, it's so nice to be in my own bed. Night night x

When Emily came back the next morning, I could see that she was relieved.

'It was so lovely to wake up in our own home with Felix in his cot next to me,' she smiled.

'Not long to wait now,' I told her.

Emily and Felix didn't have a huge amount of stuff, but every day she moved a few more of their things over to the flat.

I asked her what she'd like to do to mark her final goodbye.

'Why don't I cook you a meal at the flat?' she suggested.

'That would be lovely,' I said.

She and Felix had been spending most days there anyway and had only come back to my house to sleep.

That evening, I drove round to Emily's flat. I'd bought her a plant and framed a lovely photo I'd taken of her and Felix together.

When she answered the door, Emily looked happy and relaxed.

'Come in,' she smiled.

I looked around the flat and smiled. There was a curry bubbling away on the hob and Felix was sitting in his high chair. Weaning had been going well and he was now eating and enjoying a whole range of food that Emily had made for him. There was a bunch of flowers arranged in a glass vase on a sideboard and a scented candle burning. The living room looked totally different with its blue-and-white patterned wallpaper and the hallway was now painted a dark green.

'Gosh, it looks really lovely,' I smiled. 'It feels like a different flat.'

'That's what I was aiming for,' smiled Emily.

'I haven't shown you Felix's room yet,' she said, scooping him up out of the high chair.

The blue walls had been replaced with a mustard yellow colour with pops of red, and there was a brand-new cot.

I walked over to it and spotted something – the blue elephant blanket with Felix's name on it and the fluffy rabbit. The two things Emily had left him with in the bag when she'd abandoned him at the train station.

'I couldn't bear to throw those away,' she told me in a quiet voice. 'Somehow, I don't mind seeing them. They remind me of how far Felix and I have come.'

'And you should be so, so proud of that,' I nodded, squeezing her hand.

I hoped that, in time, she could finally forgive herself for being unwell.

Any sadness I felt about seeing them leave was soon forgotten when I saw how positive Emily was.

'I'm not going to go back to work for another few weeks,' she told me as we ate dinner together. 'Then my sister's coming over from New Zealand so I'll get to meet her baby girl and Felix can meet his cousin for the first time.'

'How are you feeling?' I asked her.

'Lucky,' she smiled. 'I don't know if the fear of that awful illness coming back will ever leave me, but we did it. I've got support for when I need it and I know who to turn to if I start to feel ill again. We got through it, Felix is with me and we're both safe and we're a little family again. That's all I could ever have wished for.'

It was a bittersweet moment as I gave Felix a goodbye cuddle that evening before I left.

'Goodbye, little man,' I told him.

He struggled in my arms, and held his hands out to Emily.

'See you soon,' I told her, giving her a hug. 'Call me anytime if you need anything.'

As I drove home that night, I thought about the shock I'd felt six months ago when I'd heard about the mum who'd abandoned her newborn baby in a bag at the train station. I never thought at the time that there was any possibility the person who had done that to their baby would ever be allowed to have him back again. I had learnt so much about mental health and how ill someone could get. It's something I'll never forget. For Emily to come back from that, and her actions when she was ill, was a huge achievement.

Emily had done the impossible and proved us all wrong, and I couldn't have been happier for her and Felix.

Author's Note

A Note on Postpartum Psychosis

Statistics show that up to 1,200 new mothers in England and Wales suffer from postpartum psychosis each year.

It's a severe but treatable form of mental illness that begins suddenly in the days and weeks following birth. Symptoms include hallucinations and delusions, often with mania, depression or confusion. It can worsen very quickly and it should always be treated as a medical emergency. For others, things can happen more gradually. Like Emily, some people who get it have no previous history of mental illness. If the mother has a history of bipolar disorder, they are thought to have a higher risk of postpartum psychosis. Almost all mums recover fully after an episode of it.

For immediate support for postpartum psychosis, please see your GP urgently, call NHS 111 or attend A&E. If you feel there is any imminent danger, call 999 and ask for an ambulance.

AUTHOR'S NOTE

For further information, help and support please contact Action on Postpartum Psychosis (www.app-network.org).

Acknowledgements

Thank you to my children, Tess, Pete and Sam, who are such a big part of my fostering today. However, I had not met you when Amena, Felix and Emily came into my home. To my wide circle of fostering friends – you know who you are! Your support and your laughter are valued. To my friend Andrew B for your continued encouragement and care. Thanks also to Heather Bishop, who spent many hours listening and enabled this story to be told, my literary agent Rowan Lawton and to Anna Valentine, Vicky Eribo and Beth Eynon at Seven Dials for giving me the opportunity to share these stories.

Photo credit: Simon Way

Maggie Hartley has fostered more than 300 children while being a foster carer for over twenty years. Taking on the children other carers often can't cope with, Maggie helps children that are deemed 'unadoptable' because of their behaviour or the extreme trauma that they've been through.

She's looked after refugees, supported children through sexual abuse and violence court cases, cared for teenagers on remand and taught young mums how to parent their newborn babies.

You can find her on Facebook at MaggieHartleyAuthor, where she would love to hear from you.

Coming soon from Maggie Hartley . . .

Don't Leave Me Here
Saskia's true story of secrets, kidnap and abuse

What possesses a mum to kidnap her own child? That's what Maggie asks herself when she's brought in to foster thirteen-year-old Saskia.

Saskia has been the subject of a bitter custody battle between her parents, but when mum, Rosa, fears the courts are going to favour her ex-husband, James, she takes matters into her own hands. With Rosa facing criminal charges, and Saskia refusing to live with her dad, her future looks uncertain.

Will Maggie be able to step in and discover the bombshell that has torn this family apart?

A powerful, moving true story from Sunday Times *bestselling author Maggie Hartley, Britain's most-loved foster carer.*

Available July 2025 in paperback, ebook and audio

'Please help me,' he said in a small voice. 'Will you help me?'

Six-year-old Ralph has only been in the care system for three days and has already been rejected by three different foster carers. After hitting a teacher at his school and causing mayhem since he arrived four months ago, staff are unable to get a hold of his mum and her partner.

Social Services are called and when Ralph turns up at Maggie's house, she knows immediately it's going to be a challenge. Within a couple of hours, Ralph has trashed Maggie's house and spit on her face. After a nightmare first day though, Maggie notices that Ralph is limping and a hospital check reveals broken limbs and several injuries that are months old. Can Maggie help this troubled little boy, who has been rejected by everyone in his life, find his forever home?

From Britain's most-loved foster carer, a powerful true story of abuse, family and hope.

**Read on for an extract from *Will You Help Me?*,
available now in paperback, ebook and audio**

Today was supposed to be a happy day but the teenage girl in my arms was sobbing her heart out.

'I miss my m-mum,' sniffed Amena. 'I w-wish she was here.'

'I know you do, flower,' I soothed, stroking her long brown hair. 'I know you do.'

I'd been fostering Amena for the past eight months and today was her sixteenth birthday. Despite being as tall as me and looking so grown up, inside she was still a little girl who wanted her mummy.

Amena and her mum, Hodan, were originally from Somalia but they'd been in the UK for several years. Hodan's sister lived in France and when she'd been diagnosed with lung cancer at the beginning of the year, Hodan had gone over there to nurse her through surgery and treatment. With no other family in the UK and not wanting to take her daughter out of school, Hodan had sought help from Social Services and that's when Amena had come into my care.

She was such a lovely girl – polite, helpful, kind – and she had been easy to have around. Whatever other placements I had, she always adapted with ease to the other children and never once complained. Amena had seen her mum a couple of times, most recently three weeks ago. It had been the school summer holidays and Hodan had managed to get the money together to get a ferry back to the UK for a week. Amena had loved seeing her mum but understandably it had really unsettled her to have to say goodbye again.

It was just the two of them and I knew that they were incredibly close. This was the first birthday Amena had spent without her mother so I understood why she was feeling upset. All I could do was give her a hug and let her cry it out.

I'd tried my best to make the morning special for her. She'd just had a breakfast of pancakes and chocolate spread, and I'd wrapped lots of little gifts like make-up, stationery and toiletries and piled them up on the kitchen table. She'd been so pleased and excited, and now it was time for her to head off to school.

'I know you're sad not to see your mum today but you can give her a call later when you get home,' I told her.

She nodded and wiped the tears from her face.

'And remember you've got your party to look forward to tonight,' I added, affectionately tucking her hair behind her ear.

'I know,' she sniffed, giving me a weak smile. 'It'll be really cool.'

It was mid-September but the weather had been so warm and sunny that Amena had invited some girls round after school to have pizza and mocktails in the garden.

Amena was the only child that I was fostering at that time so, once I'd waved her off to school, I was determined to have a productive day. Experience told me that that the peace and quiet was unlikely to last so I took the opportunity to catch up on some paperwork and life admin. Then after lunch, I started decorating the garden for Amena and her friends. I was keen to make it look lovely for her, so I hooked some fairy lights up around the patio and tied some bunches of balloons onto the fence. I'd got some plastic glasses, paper umbrellas and cocktail stirrers for their mocktails and I prepared some bowls of crisps and other nibbles. I'd bought some pizzas for later on in the evening and a chocolate birthday cake.

By 2 p.m., everything was ready and I was just admiring my handiwork when my mobile rang. It was my supervising social worker from the fostering agency that I worked for.

'Hi, Becky,' I said. 'How are you?'

'I'm OK,' she replied. 'Is now a good time to talk? What are you up to?'

I explained about Amena's party.

'That sounds nice,' she said.

She hesitated.

'I'm sorry, this is probably not a great time for me to ask you this . . .'

Instinct told me exactly what she was going to say.

'Is it about a placement?' I asked her.

'I'm afraid it is,' she sighed. 'Social Services have just called me. They're desperately searching for a placement for a six-year-old boy.'

'OK,' I told her, sitting down at the kitchen table so I could concentrate.

Becky explained that his name was Ralph and he'd come into the care system three days ago although she didn't know the circumstances yet.

'Where's he been for the past three days then?' I asked curiously.

'Well, that's the thing,' said Becky. 'Apparently he's been through two foster carers already and they've both said they couldn't cope with him and asked Social Services to take him back.'

I was immediately intrigued. I could understand a teenager causing that much disruption but what on earth could a six-year-old do to make two people give notice on him so quickly?

'The social worker only dropped him off at the second carer's house yesterday afternoon and she called Social Services an hour ago to say that she'd decided not to carry on with the placement and wouldn't be picking him up from school this afternoon,' she explained.

'Do you know why?' I asked.

'I'm afraid not,' replied Becky.

She explained that his social worker was going to go and pick him up from school.

'I think they were hoping to find a carer by the end of the school day but obviously it's been tricky as many carers are wary when they hear he's already been moved twice,' she added.

'Poor little lad,' I sighed. 'Having all those moves will be really confusing for him.'

It was always upsetting to hear when children had been moved from carer to carer. I'd fostered some children who'd had multiple moves and it was always unsettling for them.

I knew what Becky was telling me would ring alarm bells with a lot of carers and put them off. However, I liked kids that were branded as 'difficult'. I enjoyed the challenge and finding out what made them tick. In fact, it was one of the reasons I'd gone into fostering in the first place. In my twenties, I'd got a job as a deputy matron at a residential boarding school for what were described at the time as maladjusted boys. I lived on site and was on duty 24/7 during term time. It was intense and exhausting and it certainly wasn't easy, but I loved it. I liked stroppy kids and they seemed to respond well to me. When I eventually left there and started childminding, I missed the challenge.

'What do you reckon, Maggie?' asked Becky. 'Do you think you'd consider taking this little lad on?'

'I know it sounds silly but the only thing stopping me from saying yes is Amena's party,' I told her. 'She was so upset this morning about not being with her mum, and I don't want to have to call it off because I've got a new placement arriving.'

'Let me talk to the social worker and explain,' said Becky. 'It might be that she was going to take him back to the office anyway so she could bring him to you later on tonight.'

I felt awful as I didn't want to keep a six-year-old hanging around.

'If they could bring him here around 7 p.m.,' I told her. 'The girls will probably all be going by then.'

It wasn't ideal but I wanted to make sure that, given his age, Ralph was fed, bathed and ready for bed by 8 or 9 p.m. otherwise it wasn't fair on him.

'Social Services are desperate to find a placement for him so I'm sure we can sort something out,' Becky told me.

'I'll wait to hear back from you then,' I said.

It was only when I put the phone down that I suddenly questioned what I had done. This little boy must have significant behavioural problems if two carers had given up on him so quickly, but in a way it made me even more determined to help him.